MW01259676

The Biblical
Path
of Life

Year One ◆ Quarter One

© *2018 M.J. Ross*
ALL RIGHTS RESERVED

Editorial Design and book cover by **Sergio León**

Permission to copy the Q&A Sections granted
with purchase of this book.

Visit ***www.biblicalpath.com*** *for additional lesson support,*
and corresponding activity pages for children.

M.J. Ross

The Biblical Path of Life

Year One Quarter One

YEAR ONE - 1st. Quarter

Current Book

Overview of Old Testament
(Old Testament and Five Divisions):

THESE THIRTEEN LESSONS ARE CONTAINED INSIDE THIS BOOK

YEAR ONE - 2nd. Quarter

Five Books of the Law:

Genesis (Book of Beginnings);

Exodus (Book of Redemption);

Leviticus (Book of Worship);

Numbers (Book of Wanderings);

Deuteronomy (Renewed Covenant)

YEAR TWO - 1st. Quarter

Next 2 historical books:

The kingdom was divided – including their prophets.
Pre-exile:

> **I Kings 12 - 22** (Divided Kingdom),
>
> **II Kings** (Carried away as captives),
>
>> * **Hosea** (love of God in spite of spiritual adultery),
>>
>> * **Amos** (a prophet from the country),
>>
>> * **Obadiah** (warning to those who persecute Israelites),
>>
>> * **Jonah** (an unwilling/ reluctant prophet),
>>
>> * **Nahum** (Prophesied the destruction of Nineveh).

Israel (the Northern Kingdom)

Lesson 1	I Kings 12-15: Rehoboam, Jeroboam, & Divided Kingdom
Lesson 2	I Kings 16:29- 22:53: Ahab & Elijah
Lesson 3	II Kings 1 - 2: Elijah & Elisha
Lesson 4	II Kings 3 - 9:10: Elisha
Lesson 5	II Kings 9:11 – 13:9: Jehu – Jehoahaz
Lesson 6	Jonah: The Reluctant Prophet

YEAR ONE - 2nd. Quarter

Five Books of the Law:

Genesis (Book of Beginnings);

Exodus (Book of Redemption);

Leviticus (Book of Worship);

Numbers (Book of Wanderings);

Deuteronomy (Renewed Covenant)

YEAR ONE - 3rd. Quarter

First Five Historical books:
When Canaan Was Occupied before Exile:

Joshua (Conquest);

Judges (Disobedience);

Ruth (Righteousness during Judges);

1 Samuel (Transition to Monarchy);

2 Samuel (David's Rule) **and Begin 1 Kings**

YEAR ONE - 4th. Quarter

Five Personal Books:

Job (Righteous Man);

Psalms (Songs—Hymns);

Proverbs (Wisdom);

Ecclesiastes (the Preacher);

Song of Solomon (Love in Marriage)

YEAR TWO - 1st. Quarter

Next 2 historical books:
The kingdom was divided – including their prophets.
Pre-exile:

> **I Kings 12 - 22** (Divided Kingdom),
>
> **II Kings** (Carried away as captives),
>
> * **Hosea** (love of God in spite of spiritual adultery),
>
> * **Amos** (a prophet from the country),
>
> * **Obadiah** (warning to those who persecute Israelites),
>
> * **Jonah** (an unwilling/ reluctant prophet),
>
> * **Nahum** (Prophesied the destruction of Nineveh).

Israel (the Northern Kingdom)

Lesson	1	I Kings 12-15: Rehoboam, Jeroboam, & Divided Kingdom
Lesson	2	I Kings 16:29- 22:53: Ahab & Elijah
Lesson	3	II Kings 1 - 2: Elijah & Elisha
Lesson	4	II Kings 3 - 9:10: Elisha
Lesson	5	II Kings 9:11 – 13:9: Jehu – Jehoahaz
Lesson	6	Jonah: The Reluctant Prophet

* *Pre-exile Prophets*

YEAR TWO - 2nd. Quarter

Judah: Part 1:

Next 4 historical books when the kingdom was divided – including their prophet:
Pre-exile:

I Kings (Divided Kingdom),

II Kings (Carried away as captives),

I Chronicles (Spiritual perspective of kingdoms)

II Chronicles (Spiritual perspective of downfall) – beginning with the genealogy of the nation Israel and then following Judah through the time of the kings, and

* **Joel** (plague of locusts).

Judah (the Southern Kingdom):

Lesson 1 I Chronicles 1-2: Adam – Genealogy of Judah
Lesson 2 I Chronicles 3 – 10: The Beginnings of the Kings – Saul
Lesson 3 I Chronicles 11 – 20: David Becomes King
Lesson 4 I Chronicles 21 – 29: David

* *Pre-exile Prophet*

YEAR TWO - 3rd. Quarter

Judah: Part 2:

Historical books when the kingdom was divided – including their prophets:
Pre-exile:

II Kings (Carried away as captives),

II Chronicles (Spiritual perspective of downfall) – beginning with the genealogy of the nation Israel and then following Judah through the time of the kings.

* **Isaiah** (foretold of Babylonian conquest
  & Suffering Savior),
* **Jeremiah** (Weeping Prophet – foretold of "Branch"
  of David),
* **Lamentations** (Poem – by Jeremiah – of the Fall
  of Jerusalem),
* **Micah** (Prophet to both kingdom calling for people
  to "hear"),

* **Habakkuk** (Asked God why – God answered),

* **Zephaniah** (God's judgment and mercy).

* *Pre-exile Prophets*

YEAR THREE - 1st. Quarter

The Silent Years, an overview of the New Testament and the 4 Gospels:
(Matthew, Mark, Luke and John):

* **Habakkuk** (Asked God why – God answered),

* **Zephaniah** (God's judgment and mercy).

* *Pre-exile Prophets*

YEAR TWO - 4th. Quarter

Last 3 historical books, including their prophets
Post-exile:

* **Ezekiel** (foretold of "Shepherd" King),

* **Daniel** (foretold Messiah to be "cut off"),

** **Haggai** (God comes first),

** **Zechariah** (Finish – God's not finished with them yet),

** **Malachi** (last call before 400 year silence)

Lesson 1   Ezekiel 1-32: Judah's Fall

Lesson 2   Ezekiel 33-48: Judah's Future

Lesson 3   Daniel 1-4: Nebuchadnezzar, King of Babylon

Lesson 4   Daniel 5-12: Daniel, God's Man

Lesson 5   Ezra 1-5 & Haggai: Zerubbabel Begins Rebuilding the Temple

Lesson 6   Zechariah & Ezra 6: God's Plans for the Future
       & the Temple Completed

Lesson 7   Esther: A Woman Who Saved her People

Lesson 8   Ezra 7-10: Ezra Restores the Relationship

Lesson 9   Nehemiah 1-6: Rebuilding the Walls

Lesson 10   Nehemiah 7-13: Instructions for the People

* *During Exile Prophets*

** *Post-exile Prophets*

YEAR THREE - 1st. Quarter

The Silent Years, an overview of the New Testament and the 4 Gospels:
(Matthew, Mark, Luke and John):

YEAR THREE - 2nd. Quarter

The 2nd Division of the New Testament:
The History Book: Acts

YEAR THREE - 3rd. Quarter

9 Epistles to churches:
Romans, I Corinthians, II Corinthians, Galatians, Ephesians, Philippians, Colossians, I Thessalonians, II Thessalonians

YEAR THREE - 4th. Quarter

4 Epistles to preachers & 9 General Epistles:
I Timothy, II Timothy, Titus, Philemon, Hebrews, James, I Peter, II Peter, I John, II John, III John, Jude, and Revelation.

Lesson 1   I Timothy: Fight the Good Fight

Lesson 2   II Timothy: Be Faithful

Lesson 3   Titus & Philemon: Maintain Christian Living

Lesson 4   Hebrews 1 – 7: Jesus, our High Priest

Lesson 5   Hebrews 8 – 13: The Shadow Revealed

Lesson 6   James: Christians Show Faith by Works

Lesson 7   I Peter: Become Lively Stones

Lesson 8   II Peter: Growing in Grace

Lesson 9   I John: The Test of Faith: Truth vs. False

Lesson 10   II John, III John: Truth in Christian Living

Lesson 11   Jude: The Abandonment of God's Truth Revealed

Lesson 12   Revelation: The Revealing by Jesus Christ

Lesson 13   Review of the New Testament: Matthew – Revelation

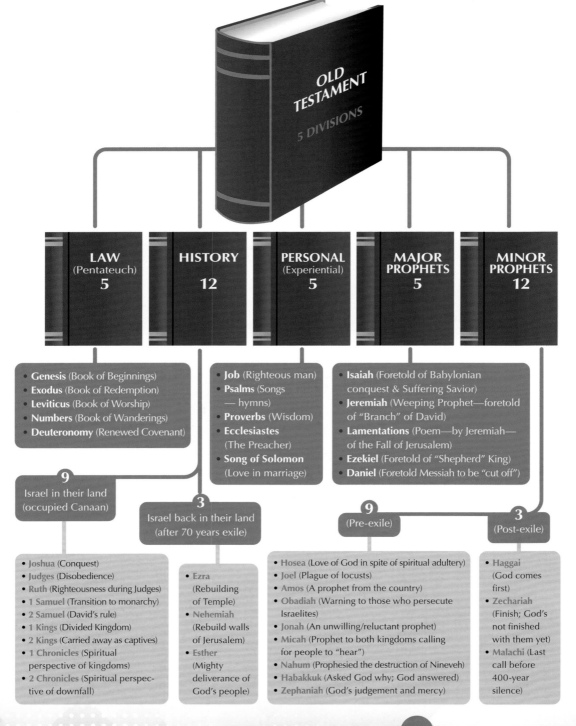

OLD TESTAMENT

5 DIVISIONS

LAW (Pentateuch) **5**

HISTORY 12

PERSONAL (Experiential) **5**

MAJOR PROPHETS 5

MINOR PROPHETS 12

- **Genesis** (Book of Beginnings)
- **Exodus** (Book of Redemption)
- **Leviticus** (Book of Worship)
- **Numbers** (Book of Wanderings)
- **Deuteronomy** (Renewed Covenant)

- **Job** (Righteous man)
- **Psalms** (Songs — hymns)
- **Proverbs** (Wisdom)
- **Ecclesiastes** (The Preacher)
- **Song of Solomon** (Love in marriage)

- **Isaiah** (Foretold of Babylonian conquest & Suffering Savior)
- **Jeremiah** (Weeping Prophet—foretold of "Branch" of David)
- **Lamentations** (Poem—by Jeremiah—of the Fall of Jerusalem)
- **Ezekiel** (Foretold of "Shepherd" King)
- **Daniel** (Foretold Messiah to be "cut off")

9
Israel in their land (occupied Canaan)

3
Israel back in their land (after 70 years exile)

9
(Pre-exile)

3
(Post-exile)

- **Joshua** (Conquest)
- **Judges** (Disobedience)
- **Ruth** (Righteousness during Judges)
- **1 Samuel** (Transition to monarchy)
- **2 Samuel** (David's rule)
- **1 Kings** (Divided Kingdom)
- **2 Kings** (Carried away as captives)
- **1 Chronicles** (Spiritual perspective of kingdoms)
- **2 Chronicles** (Spiritual perspective of downfall)

- **Ezra** (Rebuilding of Temple)
- **Nehemiah** (Rebuild walls of Jerusalem)
- **Esther** (Mighty deliverance of God's people)

- **Hosea** (Love of God in spite of spiritual adultery)
- **Joel** (Plague of locusts)
- **Amos** (A prophet from the country)
- **Obadiah** (Warning to those who persecute Israelites)
- **Jonah** (An unwilling/reluctant prophet)
- **Micah** (Prophet to both kingdoms calling for people to "hear")
- **Nahum** (Prophesied the destruction of Nineveh)
- **Habakkuk** (Asked God why; God answered)
- **Zephaniah** (God's judgement and mercy)

- **Haggai** (God comes first)
- **Zechariah** (Finish; God's not finished with them yet)
- **Malachi** (Last call before 400-year silence)

Old Testament Bookshelf

LAW

HISTORY

PERSONAL

MAJOR PROPHETS

MINOR PROPHETS

THE SEVEN DISPENSATIONS

LESSON 1

Key Verse

For by him were all things created, that are in heaven, and that are in earth, visible and invisible, whether they be thrones, or dominions, or principalities, or powers: all things were created by him, and for him:

— COLOSSIANS 1:16

Key Verse Thought: We must understand this verse before beginning the study. God created everything. He created it for Himself. God's plan was to have a relationship with mankind.

Emphasis: We must understand that we were created by God for a purpose. While God dealt with us in different ways through the ages, He created us to have a relationship with Him.

Lesson Summary: The Bible is laid out in certain time frames, also called dispensations. A dispensation is the method in which God deals with mankind throughout the ages because of mankind's sin and in God's divine government. Each of the dispensations may be regarded as a new test of the natural man, and each ends in judgment, marking his utter failure in every dispensation. It is with that thought that we will look at the scriptures as a whole.

This week we will see how the Bible is laid out from beginning to end. We will understand that God dealt with His creation in different ways at different times. God created the world as perfect, but man sinned, bringing the judgment of death into the world. Throughout the ages, God gave individuals many opportunities to have a relationship with Him, but each time they failed. They had to understand that the only way that relationship could ever be restored would be by the atoning death of His Son, Jesus. We will try to see how God dealt with man throughout the dispensations and how God worked to bring man back to Him.

Suggested Bible Reading to Prepare for This Lesson

- ⊘ Monday: **Genesis 1–3**
- ⊘ Tuesday: **Genesis 4–8**
- ⊘ Wednesday: **Genesis 9–11**
- ⊘ Thursday: **Genesis 12–24**
- ⊘ Friday: **Exodus 12–16; Deuteronomy 28–31**
- ⊘ Saturday: **John 1–3; Matthew 24–25; Revelation 19–20**

The Seven Dispensations

① First Dispensation

- The dispensation of innocence
- From the creation of man to the fall and expulsion

② Second Dispensation

- The dispensation of conscience
- From the expulsion from Eden to the flood

③ Third Dispensation

- The dispensation of human government
- From the flood to the dispersion at Babel

④ Fourth Dispensation

- The dispensation of promise
- From the call of Abraham to the Egyptian bondage

5 Fifth Dispensation

- The dispensation of the Law
- From the exodus to the death of Jesus on the cross

6 Sixth Dispensation

- The dispensation of grace
- From Jesus's resurrection to the Second Coming of Christ

7 Seventh Dispensation

- The dispensation of the kingdom
- From the judgment of the nations to the New Jerusalem

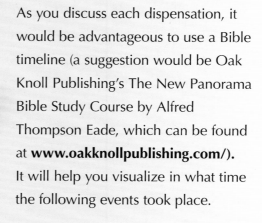

SPECIAL NOTE

As you discuss each dispensation, it would be advantageous to use a Bible timeline (a suggestion would be Oak Knoll Publishing's The New Panorama Bible Study Course by Alfred Thompson Eade, which can be found at **www.oakknollpublishing.com/).** It will help you visualize in what time the following events took place.

First Dispensation
Genesis 1–3

The Dispensation of Innocence

God created a perfect universe. His crowning creation was man, created in the image of God. He placed the first man, Adam, in a perfect garden with all of the species He had created. He then instructed Adam about his responsibilities: "And God blessed them, and God said unto them, Be fruitful, and multiply, and replenish the earth, and subdue it: and have dominion over the fish of the sea, and over the fowl of the air, and over every living thing that moveth upon the earth" (Genesis 1:28). God then declared that it was very good. Within this perfect world, they were free to eat of anything in the garden. "And God said, Behold, I have given you every herb bearing seed, which is upon the face of all the earth, and every tree, in the which is the fruit of a tree yielding seed; to you it shall be for meat" (Genesis 1:29). There was only one exception: "16. And the LORD God commanded the man, saying, Of every tree of the garden thou mayest freely eat: 17. But of the tree of the knowledge of good and evil, thou shalt not eat of it: for in the day that thou eatest thereof thou shalt surely die" (Genesis 2:16–17).

It is here that we see Satan enter the picture in the form of a serpent. He twisted the Word of God, deceiving Eve. "And Adam was not deceived, but the woman being deceived was in the transgression" (1 Timothy 2:14). She took of the fruit of the tree of the knowledge of good and evil, and then she gave it to Adam, who was not deceived but took of it willingly. It was then that their eyes were opened. "And the eyes of them both were opened, and they knew that they were naked; and they sewed fig leaves together, and made themselves aprons" (Genesis 3:7). They recognized they had sinned. Because of their sin, there was immediate separation from God. They then hid from God. God cursed the serpent because he caused the sin, and at the same time God gave Satan his everlasting judgment of eternal separation from God. Then God gave a warning and a promise of hope to all of mankind: "And I will put enmity between thee and the woman, and between thy seed and her seed; it shall bruise thy head, and thou shalt bruise his heel" (Genesis 3:15). There would be a constant conflict between Satan and mankind—forever. But God promised that the war was won from this point. For He promised to send One to deliver mankind from Satan and the punishment for sin (death; see Romans 6:23) forever.

Satan twisted the Word of God, deceiving Eve.

It was then that God cursed humans for their sin (see Genesis 3:16–19). Then God kicked them out of the Garden of Eden forever, placing an angel with a flaming sword to guard it.

We call this The Fall. But remember: God gave a promise of redemption.

The first dispensation ended with judgment—the expulsion from the garden.

Second Dispensation
Genesis 4–8

The Dispensation of Conscience

We remember the events of the conflict between Cain and Abel (see Genesis 4:2–26), along with the tragedy of the first murder (of Abel) and the rejection of God by a man (Cain). From here we see a definite delineation between those who follow God and those who choose to please themselves. The lineage of Seth, born to Adam and Eve, shows a renewal of the righteous seed lost in Abel's death. The seed of Cain becomes continually wicked, and the wickedness covers the earth until "… GOD saw that the wickedness of man was great in the earth, and that every imagination of the thoughts of his heart was only evil continually" (Genesis 6:5). God was grieved in His heart, and He then decided to destroy the whole earth. "But Noah found grace in the eyes of the LORD" (Genesis 6:8). Noah and his family obeyed the Word of the Lord, built an ark, and were spared.

The seed of Cain becomes continually wicked.

The second dispensation ended with judgment—the flood.

Third Dispensation
Genesis 9–11

The Dispensation of Human Government

Noah and his family left the ark after the flood. "And God blessed Noah and his sons, and said unto them, Be fruitful, and multiply, and replenish the earth" (Genesis 9:1). God then proceeded to establish the "law of the land." God gave man specifics to institute a human government with man now being responsible for governing the world (see Genesis 9:1–11). God promised to never destroy the earth again by water. Humans now needed to govern themselves, but they failed. Although mankind began to replenish the world, they remained together. "And they said, Go to, let us build us a city and a tower, whose top may reach unto heaven; and let us make us a name, lest we be scattered abroad upon the face of the whole earth" (Genesis 11:4). They did not want to replenish the whole world. Instead, they wanted to remain together, seeking to make for themselves a great name. There is that enmity again— choosing the will of individuals over the will of God. God then confused their language, forcing them to separate and replenish the whole earth.

God promise never to destroy again the earth by water.

The third dispensation ended with judgment—the dispersion at Babel.

Fourth Dispensation

The Dispensation of Promise

With the dispersal of the people came a forsaking of God. In that, we see a rise and spread of idolatry throughout the earth. It was during that time that God chose a family to separate from the rest of the idolaters. God called Abram to leave his family and walk throughout a land that God would give to him, making of him a great nation. In that call, God made a promise and covenant with Abram that, through him, all the families of the earth would be blessed. "**1.** Now the LORD had said unto Abram, Get thee out of thy country, and from thy kindred, and from thy father's house, unto a land that I will shew thee: **2.** And I will make of thee a great

God fulfilled His promise to Abraham giving him a son, Isaac

nation, and I will bless thee, and make thy name great; and thou shalt be a blessing: **3.** And I will bless them that bless thee, and curse him that curseth thee: and in thee shall all families of the earth be blessed" (Genesis 12:1–3).

Abram obeyed God. Although Abram (later renamed Abraham) and his wife, Sarai (later renamed Sarah), were old and had no children, they believed and trusted God. God fulfilled His promise, giving them a son, Isaac. Isaac married and had twin boys, Esau and Jacob. Jacob (later renamed Israel) married and had twelve sons (which became the twelve tribes of Israel). Joseph, Jacob's favorite of the twelve sons, was hated by his brothers. They sold Joseph into slavery. Years later, when there was a great famine in the land, Joseph was able to bring his family to Egypt, where he had become a great ruler, and to save them. They remained in Egypt until there was a king who did not know Joseph. "8. Now there arose up a new king over Egypt, which knew not Joseph. 9. And he said unto his people, Behold, the people of the children of Israel are more and mightier than we" (Exodus 1:8–9). He became fearful that they would rise up and revolt against the Egyptians. The pharaoh oppressed the people and then began to kill their newborn male children.

The fourth dispensation began with a promise but ended with bondage and oppression.

Fifth Dispensation

The Dispensation of Law

God's people were in bondage in Egypt. But God heard and rose up a mighty deliverer, Moses. He was a baby saved from the pharaoh's fate of death in the river yet raised in Pharaoh's house. After forty years, once he decided to side with his people, he left Egypt. He remained in the desert for another forty years until God called him from a burning bush. Moses then returned to Egypt and, by the power of God, demanded that Pharaoh let God's people go. Pharaoh refused, but after ten great plagues, he finally agreed to let God's people go. The tenth plague was an institution of the Passover, the death of the firstborn, showing the mighty deliverance God would give. The Israelites were to kill a lamb for each house and sprinkle the blood on the doorposts. The death angel would then pass over each house with the blood. When Pharaoh conceded and said they could leave, the people did so. They passed through the Red Sea on dry land, but Pharaoh's army, following them, drowned. The people then went to the foot of Mount Sinai. They remained camped there while Moses went up the mount and received the Law, including the Ten Commandments, from God. It was during their encampment at Sinai that they were organized and numbered as a people by tribe. When they reached the brink of the Promised Land (the land promised to Abraham and his descendants), they sent twelve spies into the land. Ten brought back a report of fear and defeat, while two brought back words of encouragement that the land could be conquered. The people believed the ten, and that generation wandered in the desert for forty years and died without ever receiving the promise. Their children would be the generation to enter into the Promised Land.

After the death of Moses, Joshua was appointed to lead the people into the Promised Land. After the land was conquered, it was then divided by tribes and given to the people. "And the people served the LORD all the days of Joshua, and all the days of the elders that outlived Joshua, who had seen all the great works of the LORD, that he did for Israel" (Judges 2:7). The people served the Lord while Joshua lived, but after his death and after the men who served with him died, the people began a cycle of backsliding. God would send a judge to deliver them, and they would forsake God again. The words in Judges 17:6 declare it the best: "In those days *there was* no king in Israel, *but* every man did *that which was* right in his own eyes."

After many years of this vicious cycle, the people told Samuel, the last judge, that they demanded a king. "And said unto him, Behold, thou art old, and thy sons walk not in thy ways: now make us a king to judge us like all the nations" (1 Samuel 8:5). God told Samuel to give them a king. The first king was Saul. He was everything the people thought they wanted in a king, and Saul ruled for forty years. But Saul disobeyed God, so God rejected him and even his family as king. God then chose David. Read what Acts 13:22 says about David: "And when he had removed him, he raised up unto them David to be their king; to whom also he gave testimony, and said, I have found David the son of Jesse, a man after mine own heart, which shall fulfil all my will."

David conquered the land and had the greatest kingdom that Israel ever had. He ruled for forty years, and upon his death, his

They passed through the Red Sea on dry land.

son, Solomon, became king of Israel. He, too, ruled for forty years. Solomon was the wisest and wealthiest king. He built the temple of the Lord that his father, David, had prepared. But Solomon allowed his heart to be taken from God, and he built high places on all of the hills around Jerusalem for idols. Because of this great apostasy, the kingdom was divided after his death. His son Rehoboam ruled over only two tribes—Judah, in the south. Jeroboam ruled over the

other ten tribes—Israel, in the north. The northern kingdom never had a good king, for they worshiped idols. They were taken captive by the Assyrians after 250 years. Judah had a few good kings and several revivals, where the people turned their hearts back to God. But 135 years after the fall of Israel, Judah was taken captive by Babylon. The city was destroyed, the temple razed, the walls broken down, and the gates burned. The people were held captive for seventy years, during which time Daniel rose in great favor with many of the kings. Cyrus issued a decree allowing the Israelites to return to their homeland to rebuild the temple. There were three movements where some of the people returned to the land of Israel. Zerubbabel led the first group back to rebuild the temple. Ezra led the second group back

King David ruled for forty years and had the greatest kingdom that Israel ever had.

in order to reestablish the Law of Moses and the religious system. Nehemiah led a small company with the plan to rebuild the city walls and gates. The walls and gates were completed in record time. During the kingdoms, the captivity, and the return, God sent many prophets to speak to the people.

At the end of Old Testament times, the Persians were the dominant rulers, yet when the New Testament time began after about four hundred years of silence from God, the Romans had become the dominant rulers. As we begin the time frame of the New Testament, we see the fulfillment of the promise God had made in Genesis 3:15 to send One who could free mankind from the penalty of sin, which was death. Jesus led a perfect life and died an atoning death. He was buried and conquered death, rising again on the third day. He became the Passover sacrifice for any who would believe.

The fifth dispensation ended in judgment of sin—
the death of Jesus on the cross.

After about four hundred years of silence from God, the Romans had become the dominant rulers.

Sixth Dispensation

The Dispensation of Grace

After Jesus's resurrection, He showed Himself alive for forty days. He then ascended into heaven after instructing His people to go and tell, making disciples. One hundred twenty people waited in the upper room until the day of Pentecost, where they were filled with the Holy Spirit that Jesus had promised. Peter preached Jesus. "Then they that gladly received his word were baptized: and the same day there were added unto them about three thousand souls" (Acts 2:41). The church was established. Peter primarily preached to the Jews, and Paul mainly preached to the Gentiles. During great persecution, the people took the gospel message with them as they fled. This allowed the news of Jesus to spread into the world, just as Jesus had commanded them.

That is the Christian's job even today—to proclaim the good news of Jesus to the lost world. The age of grace will end when Jesus comes in the clouds and calls all Christians home into heaven with Him (1 Thessalonians 4:16–17). The Spirit of God will then be removed (for the Holy Spirit dwells within believers), and this will allow the Antichrist to make his appearance (2 Thessalonians 2:4–8). After seven years of tribulation, which will include the great battle of Armageddon, the armies of the Antichrist will be destroyed, and the devil, the serpent, will be bound and imprisoned for a thousand years. All nations will then be judged by Christ on His throne.

The sixth dispensation will end in the judgment—the wine-press of His wrath (Revelation 14:19).

Seventh Dispensation

The Dispensation of the Kingdom

Jesus is now King of kings and Lord of lords. He will renew the earth to its former glory without the curse. There will be a peaceful reign that will last for a thousand years. At the end of that time, Satan will be loose for a season but then will be cast into the lake of fire to live forever. The great white throne judgment will be at this time, where all of the dead will stand before the Lord. "12. And I saw the dead, small and great, stand before God; and the books were opened: and another book was opened, which is the book of life: and the dead were judged out of those things which were written in the books, according to their works … 15. And whosoever was not found written in the book of life was cast into the lake of fire." (Revelation 20:12, 15).

There will be a peaceful reign that will last for a thousand years.

The dispensation of the kingdom ends with the final judgment at the great white throne.

Reinforcement:

The seven dispensations allow us to see how God worked among the people through the years. What began as a face-to-face relationship with God quickly turned to a sinful people unable to approach God. But God, through His grace and mercy, promised to make available to man the opportunity to once again have a relationship with Him. We see how man fell and was punished and then how all of mankind was only evil continually, so that God destroyed all but one family. God then gave the governing responsibilities to mankind, and they blew it again, causing God to confuse their language. When God selected a family, they ended up in bondage and needed God to deliver them from Pharaoh. Yet

when God laid the Promised Land out in front of them, they were afraid to go. Once they entered, they forsook God and needed judges to deliver them from the judgment God sent.

They then believed they needed a king "like the nations around" to rule them, once again rejecting God and His plan. The kingship they wanted ended with the people in captivity because they did not heed the prophets God sent to warn them. When God allowed them to return, there was great sadness, for they were not the great nation God had intended for them to be. When God sent His Son, Jesus, the fulfillment of the promise was given, if only one would believe. Jesus did many works to reveal God to the people and then laid down His life for our sins. He restored that broken relationship that nothing else through the centuries could do. When Jesus lived again, He sent His disciples to tell the world, allowing His apostles to do mighty works to help establish the church.

Although the time of the mighty works has passed, today God still uses His people to witness to a lost and dying world. We must continue this task, awaiting the day Jesus returns, when the seventh dispensation will begin.

Closing:

It would be good to close with a short prayer reinforcing today's lesson. Always include any prayer requests you may have. *Today, pray that we will be faithful to tell of the mighty work Jesus did in restoring the relationship with God that was broken at the beginning of time.*

The Seven Dispensations

Match the following:

1 ☐ First Dispensation

a. The dispensation of promise
From the call of Abraham to the Egyptian bondage.

2 ☐ Second Dispensation

b. The dispensation of the kingdom
From the judgment of the nations to
the New Jerusalem.

3 ☐ Third Dispensation

c. The dispensation of innocence
From the creation of man to the fall and expulsion

4 ☐ Fourth Dispensation

d. The dispensation of grace
From Pentecost to the Second Coming of Christ.

5 ☐ Fifth Dispensation

e. The dispensation of human government
From the flood to the dispersion at Babel.

6 ☐ Sixth Dispensation

f. The dispensation of conscience
From the expulsion from Eden to the flood.

7 ☐ Seventh Dispensation

g. The dispensation of the Law
From the exodus to the death of Jesus on the cross.

Answers: 1. c; 2. f; 3. e; 4. a; 5. g; 6. d; 7. b

GOD MADE ME

LESSON 2

Key Verse

All things were made by him; and without him was not any thing made that was made.

— JOHN 1:3

Key Verse Thought: List the five greatest things God has made (or, if in a group setting, have a general discussion, and then list the top five of the consensus of the class). Focus on the fact that the greatest thing God created was mankind. Emphasize that we are God's greatest creation, for God created man in His image. God made each and every one of us.

Emphasis: Recognize that God created us for fellowship with Him. Because sin separated man from God, we must trust Jesus to reconcile us, restoring that relationship.

Lesson Summary: God created the world and everything in it, especially man. Man disobeyed God, which caused separation, and individuals could no longer fellowship with God as before because of this separation. But God promised One would come to bridge the gap between sinful humans and God.

When was that promise fulfilled?

How did God intend us to be?

How does God want us to live?

Suggested Bible Reading to Prepare for This Lesson

- ⊘ Monday: **Psalm 139**
- ⊘ Tuesday: **Genesis 1–4**
- ⊘ Wednesday: **Galatians 4**
- ⊘ Thursday: **1 Corinthians 15**
- ⊘ Friday: **Romans 5**
- ⊘ Saturday: **Acts 17**

God Made Me

1   God Made Me

- God created the universe and everything in it (Genesis 1–2).
- Man was created in righteousness and holiness (Genesis 1:26–28; Ephesians 1:4).
- Why did God create man? (Ephesians 2:10; Luke 1:74–75; Revelation 4:11).

2   Separation from God—Sin (Disobedience)

- Man disobeyed God's command (Genesis 3:6–8).
- Man was spiritually and physically separated (Genesis 3:22–24).

3   How to Be Reconciled—Jesus Promised

- Genesis 3:15.
- Fulfilled in Jesus (Titus 2:11–15).

4   How Does God Want Me to Live, and What Does He Want us Me to Know?

- How to live
- To know His Word
- To talk with Him; have a relationship with Him

1. God Made Me

Genesis 1–2: All things were created in six days, and on the seventh day, God rested.

- Day one: light divided from darkness (Genesis 1:3–5)
- Day two: separated the waters; made the heavens (Genesis 1:6–8)
- Day three: dry land separated from the waters; created all plants (Genesis 1:9–13)
- Day four: sun (to rule the day), moon (to rule the night) and stars (Genesis 1:14–19)
- Day five: all sea life and fowls of the air (Genesis 1:20–23)
- Day six: all of the animals that live on land, and man (Genesis 1:24–31)

The world was formed by God. He created everything (see Genesis 1). The crowning glory of his creation was man, which He created in His own image. "26. And God said, Let us make man in our image, after our likeness: and let them have dominion over the fish of the sea, and over the fowl of the air, and over the cattle, and over all the earth, and over every creeping thing that creepeth upon the earth. 27. So God created man in his own image, in the image of God created he him; male and female created he them" (Genesis 1:26–27).

Man was created without sin—sinless, just like God. God created man in righteousness and holiness. "According as he hath chosen us in him before the foundation of the world, that we should be holy and without blame before him in love" (Ephesians 1:4). God talked with man in the garden. "And they heard the voice of the LORD God walking in the garden in the cool of the day..." (Genesis 3:8a). God met with man to fellowship with him.

Why did God create man? From the beginning of time, God wanted man to walk with Him. "For we are his workmanship, created in Christ Jesus unto good works, which God hath before ordained that we should walk in them" (Ephesians 2:10).

He wants man to serve Him. "74. That he would grant unto us, that we being delivered out of the hand of our enemies might serve him without fear, 75. In holiness and righteousness before him, all the days of our life" (Luke 1:74–75).

God created man for His pleasure, "Thou art worthy, O Lord, to receive glory and honour and power: for thou hast created all things, and for thy pleasure they are and were created" (Revelation 4:11).

A Deeper Path:

Read Psalm 139:1–18. Understand just how special and individually God made each of us. Also be encouraged to see that God loves each person who belongs to Him and knows each of them (Psalm 139:1) and that God is always with them (Psalm 139:7–12).

God knew Jeremiah before he was even born. "Before I formed thee in the belly I knew thee; and before thou camest forth out of the womb I sanctified thee, and I ordained thee a prophet unto the nations" (Jeremiah 1:5).

2. Separation from God — Sin (Disobedience)

God told man not to eat of one fruit in the garden. "16. And the LORD God commanded the man, saying, Of every tree of the garden thou mayest freely eat: 17. But of the tree of the knowledge of good and evil, thou shalt not eat of it: for in the day that thou eatest thereof thou shalt surely die" (Genesis 2:16–17). But they disobeyed.

> 6. And when the woman saw that the tree was good for food, and that it was pleasant to the eyes, and a tree to be desired to make one wise, she took of the fruit thereof, and did eat, and gave also unto her husband with her; and he did eat. 7. And the eyes of them both were opened, and they knew that they were naked; and they sewed fig leaves together, and made themselves aprons. 8. And they heard the voice of the LORD God walking in the garden in the cool of the day: and Adam and his wife hid themselves from the presence of the LORD God amongst the trees of the garden. (Genesis 3:6–8)

When man disobeyed God's command, it separated him from God. Adam and Eve hid from God. When confronted with their disobedience, they could have confessed their sin. Instead, they passed the blame (see Genesis 3:9–21).

When man fell (sinned), his spirit was changed. Before, he met with God in the cool of the day. When he sinned, man fled from God because he now loved evil more than righteousness. "19. And this is the condemnation, that light is come into the world, and men loved darkness rather than light, because their deeds were evil. 20. For every one that doeth evil hateth the light, neither cometh to the light, lest his deeds should be reproved" (John 3:19–20). Man was no longer perfect as when God created him, no longer innocent. He died spiritually. Man no longer possessed the same godlike character.

Because God is perfect and holy, He cannot have sinful man in His presence. There was now a separation between God and man. God cast man from His presence and out of the beautiful garden He had created for man. "22. And the LORD God said, Behold, the man is become as one of us, to know good and evil: and now, lest he put forth his hand, and take also of the tree of life, and eat, and live for ever: 23. Therefore the LORD God sent him forth from the garden of Eden, to till the ground from whence he was taken. 24. So he drove out the man; and he placed at the east of the garden of Eden Cherubims, and a flaming sword which turned every way, to keep the way of the tree of life" (Genesis 3:22–24).

Men loved darkness rather than light, for his deeds were evil.

3. How to Be Reconciled — Jesus Promised

"And I will put enmity between thee and the woman, and between thy seed and her seed; it shall bruise thy head, and thou shalt bruise his heel" (Genesis 3:15). This is a promise of Jesus.

Jesus came to destroy the work of Satan. "He that committeth sin is of the devil; for the devil sinneth from the beginning. For this purpose the Son of God was manifested, that he might destroy the works of the devil" (1 John 3:8). Jesus came to restore that broken fellowship and allow us to be changed back into the same image we once were before sin entered the world.

- "But we all, with open face beholding as in a glass the glory of the Lord, are changed into the same image from glory to glory, even as by the Spirit of the Lord" (2 Corinthians 3:18).
- "And that ye put on the new man, which after God is created in righteousness and true holiness" (Ephesians 4:24).
- "And have put on the new man, which is renewed in knowledge after the image of him that created him" (Colossians 3:10).

How is this done? "11. For the grace of God that bringeth salvation hath appeared to all men, 12. Teaching us that, denying ungodliness and worldly lusts, we should live soberly, righteously, and godly, in this present world; 13. Looking for that blessed hope, and the glorious appearing of the great God and our Saviour Jesus Christ; 14. Who gave himself for us, that he might redeem us from all iniquity, and purify unto himself a peculiar people, zealous of good works. 15. These things speak, and exhort, and rebuke with all authority. Let no man despise thee" (Titus 2:11–15). That is why God promised Jesus – to "redeem us from all iniquity."

By God's grace, all people have the opportunity to be saved. Jesus allowed that relationship with God to be restored. We can now fellowship with God. How? When we read God's Word, we can hear from God. When we pray, we are talking to God. We need to have those lines of communication open. He then teaches us. He wants us to please Him in all that we do.

All people have the opportunity to be saved. Jesus allowed that relationship with God to be restored.

To Serve Him

- "74. That he would grant unto us, that we being delivered out of the hand of our enemies might serve him without fear, 75. In holiness and righteousness before him, all the days of our life" (Luke 1:74–75).

To Know His Word

- "Thy word have I hid in mine heart, that I might not sin against thee" (Psalm 119:11).
- "Study to shew thyself approved unto God, a workman that needeth not to be ashamed, rightly dividing the word of truth" (2 Timothy 2:15).
- "16. All scripture is given by inspiration of God, and is profitable for doctrine, for reproof, for correction, for instruction in righteousness: 17. That the man of God may be perfect, thoroughly furnished unto all good works" (2 Timothy 3:16–17).

To Be Like Him

- "And that ye put on the new man, which after God is created in righteousness and true holiness" (Ephesians 4:24).

To Communicate with Him

- "Call unto me, and I will answer thee, and shew thee great and mighty things, which thou knowest not" (Jeremiah 33:3).
- "He shall call upon me, and I will answer him: I will be with him in trouble; I will deliver him, and honour him" (Psalm 91:15).
- "Then shalt thou call, and the LORD shall answer; thou shalt cry, and he shall say, Here I *am*..." (Isaiah 58:9a).
- "... they shall call on my name, and I will hear them: I will say, It is my people: and they shall say, The LORD is my God" (Zechariah 13:9b).

God visits those who belong to Him each day to see how they are doing.

A Deeper Path

Understand that God visits those who belong to Him each day to see how they are doing in their walk with Him. "17. What is man, that thou shouldest magnify him? and that thou shouldest set thine heart upon him? 18. And that thou shouldest visit him every morning, and try him every moment?" (Job 7:17–18).

Try means "to prove, test, examine, search out, purify, to look out, to watch. The word suggests an investigation to determine the essential qualities, especially integrity."

Reinforcement:

If you are in a group study, have the students reconsider their unique differences yet their remarkable similarities as they consider that God made them too. Understand that God made each person unique and different from anyone else, and He has a plan for each life!

Closing:

It would be good to close with a short prayer, reinforcing today's lesson. Always include any prayer requests you may have. *Today, pray that we will recognize that God made us, and God made us to fellowship with Him. Pray that we will recognize the need for Jesus in our hearts, for only He can reconcile us to God.*

NOTE

We have always heard Jesus was the One promised from the beginning (Genesis 3:15). We will spend the next few months seeing how the Bible fits together, and we will follow the lineage of Christ throughout history.

LESSON 2

God Made Me

Read Genesis 1–2 to answer the following:

1. What was created on day one?_____

_____

_____

2. What was created on day two?_____

_____

_____

3. What was created on day thee?_____

_____

_____

4. What was created on day four?_____

_____

5. What was created on day five? _____

_____

6. What was created on day six?

_____

_____

7. Why did God create man? Ephesians 2:10 _____

_____

Luke 1:74–75 _____

Revelation 4:11 _____

8. What separated man from God? Genesis 3:6–8 _____

_____

9. What did God promise? Genesis 3:15 _____

_____

and Titus 2:11–15 _____

10. What are we to do? Psalm 119:11 _____

_____

2 Timothy 2:15 _____

Ephesians 4:24 _____

Answers:
1. light divided from darkness—light He called day and the dark He called night;
2. separated the waters; made the heavens;
3. gathered the waters together calling them Seas, dry land separated from the waters; created all plants and trees;
4. Sun, moon, and stars;
5. Sea creatures and every winged fowl;
6. every living creature and creeping thing on land, and man was created in God's image;
7. God wanted man to walk with Him; He wants man to serve Him; for His pleasure;
8. When man disobeyed God's command, sin;
9. Jesus; God promised Jesus – to give Himself to "redeem us from all iniquity";
10. Hide God's Word in our heart so we won't sin; study God's Word; allow God's Word to correct our hearts and lives so we can live for Him.)

WHY IS THE HISTORY IMPORTANT?

Key Verse

Now all these things happened unto them for ensamples: and they are written for our admonition, upon whom the ends of the world are come.

— 1 CORINTHIANS 10:11

Key Verse Thought: After reading the verse together, focus on the fact that God's Word was written for us to show us a picture of His plan. We are to learn from what is written in His Word. Each Bible "story" we have learned through the years is just a piece of the "puzzle" to complete the picture of God's plan. History may appear boring, but we are going to show how fascinating, and especially important, it is in our lives.

Emphasis: To not only recognize that history is important but to desire to know the history, just as Peter, Stephen, and Paul knew it. The history is there to help us better understand and know Jesus.

Lesson Summary: God had a plan. In the Old Testament, men didn't fully understand what that plan was, but through faith, they believed. In the New Testament, God's plan was revealed through His Son, Jesus. Men still didn't understand until Jesus died, resurrected, and ascended into heaven. But once they understood, they could not keep silent. They shared what they learned with others so they could know of God's wonderful plan as well.

Today, we will learn as Peter preached the Old Testament history and the response he received. Then we will remember Stephen as he preached the same history and the very different response to his message. Finally, we will see Saul (later called Paul), who was transformed after Stephen's preaching and how he became a mighty preacher and teacher of the history, revealing Jesus.

Suggested Bible Reading to Prepare for This Lesson

- ⊘ Monday: **Deuteronomy 6**
- ⊘ Tuesday: **Acts 2–3**
- ⊘ Wednesday: **Acts 6–7**
- ⊘ Thursday: **John 5**
- ⊘ Friday: **1 Corinthians 10**
- ⊘ Saturday: **Hebrews 12**

Why Is the History Important?

1   **Peter preached the history.**

- Jesus was the son of David, who was to rule and reign (Acts 2:22–36).
- Peter preached at the temple (Acts 3:13–26).

2   **Stephen preached the history before he was martyred.**

- He started with Abraham, Isaac, and Jacob (Acts 7:2–8).
- He continued with Joseph (Acts 7:9–18).
- He continued with Moses, bringing it to Jesus (Acts 7:19–50).
- He challenged them (Acts 7:51–53), and they rejected (Acts 7:54–60).

3   **Paul – from agreeing to Stephen's death to understanding and preaching the history himself.**

- He agreed to Stephen's death and then began persecuting believers.
- He received Christ and began preaching.
- He taught that the history in the Bible was written as our example.

1. Peter preached the history.

Peter walked with Jesus, learned from Jesus, and put his trust in Jesus. When Jesus died on the cross, Peter was scared. He didn't know what to do, so he hid. He didn't understand what had happened. He was confused. But when Jesus was alive again and came to speak with the disciples, Peter began to understand. On the day of Pentecost, Jesus sent the promised comforter (the Holy Spirit; see Acts 2). This was the last thing Jesus promised them before He ascended into heaven. Then, all of the "stories" Peter had heard, all of Jesus's teachings, began to fit together like pieces in a puzzle. Jesus came to die for man's sins. It had been taught from the beginning; he just hadn't understood until now.

Once the pieces began to fit together and Peter understood, he got excited. He preached to the people the things that he now understood. Part of that sermon follows:

22. Ye men of Israel, hear these words; Jesus of Nazareth, a man approved of God among you by miracles and wonders and signs, which God did by him in the midst of you, as ye yourselves also know: 23. Him, being delivered by the determinate counsel and foreknowledge of God, ye have taken, and by wicked hands have crucified and slain: 24. Whom God hath raised up, having loosed the pains of death: because it was not possible that he should be holden of it. 25. For David speaketh concerning him, I foresaw the Lord always before my face, for he is on

my right hand, that I should not be moved: 26. Therefore did my heart rejoice, and my tongue was glad; moreover also my flesh shall rest in hope: 27. Because thou wilt not leave my soul in hell, neither wilt thou suffer thine Holy One to see corruption. 28. Thou hast made known to me the ways of life; thou shalt make me full of joy with thy countenance. 29. Men and brethren, let me freely speak unto you of the patriarch David, that he is both dead and buried, and his sepulchre is with us unto this day. 30. Therefore being a prophet, and knowing that God had sworn with an oath to him, that of the fruit of his loins, according to the flesh, he would raise up Christ to sit on his throne; 31. He seeing this before spake of the resurrection of Christ, that his soul was not left in hell, neither his flesh did see corruption. 32. This Jesus hath God raised up, whereof we all are witnesses. 33. Therefore being by the right hand of God exalted, and having received of the Father the promise of the Holy Ghost, he hath shed forth this, which ye now see and hear. 34. For David is not ascended into the heavens: but he saith himself, The LORD said unto my Lord, Sit thou on my right hand, 35. Until I make thy foes thy footstool. 36. Therefore let all the house of Israel know assuredly, that God hath made that same Jesus, whom ye have crucified, both Lord and Christ. (Acts 2:22–36)

He understood that Jesus was the son of David, who was to rule and reign. About three thousand were saved after this sermon. "Then they that gladly received his word were baptized: and the same day there were added unto them about three thousand souls" (Acts 2:41).

At the temple gate, Peter and John healed a lame man. Peter began to preach again. He told that the God of Abraham, Isaac, and Jacob had glorified His Son, Jesus. God had showed them this through the prophets of old, yet the people did not see it. Repent! Believe in Jesus, the One whom Moses, Samuel, and all the prophets told them would come. Turn from your sins and believe in Jesus, God's Son.

11. And as the lame man which was healed held Peter and John, all the people ran together unto them in the porch that is called Solomon's, greatly wondering. 12. And when Peter saw it, he answered unto the people, Ye men of Israel, why marvel ye at this? or why look ye so earnestly on us, as though by our own power or holiness we had made this man to walk? 13. The God of Abraham, and of Isaac, and of Jacob, the God of our fathers, hath glorified his Son Jesus; whom ye delivered up, and denied him in the presence of Pilate, when he was determined to let him go. 14. But ye denied the Holy One and the Just, and desired a murderer to be granted unto you; 15. And killed the Prince of life, whom God hath raised from the dead; whereof we are witnesses. 16. And his name through faith in his name hath made this man strong, whom ye see and know: yea, the faith which is by him hath given him this perfect soundness in the presence of you all. 17. And now, brethren, I wot that through ignorance ye did it, as did also your rulers.

18. But those things, which God before had shewed by the mouth of all his prophets, that Christ should suffer, he hath so fulfilled. 19. Repent ye therefore, and be converted, that your sins may be blotted out, when the times of refreshing shall come from the presence of the Lord; 20. And he shall send Jesus Christ, which before was preached unto you: 21. Whom the heaven must receive until the times of restitution of all things, which God hath spoken by the mouth of all his holy prophets since the world began. 22. For Moses truly said unto the fathers, A prophet shall the Lord your God raise up unto you of your brethren, like unto me; him shall ye hear in all things whatsoever he shall say unto you. 23. And it shall come to pass, that every soul, which will not hear that prophet, shall be destroyed from among the people. 24. Yea, and all the prophets from Samuel and those that follow after, as many as have spoken, have likewise foretold of these days. 25. Ye are the children of the prophets, and of the covenant which God made with our fathers, saying unto Abraham, And in thy seed shall all the kindreds of the earth be blessed. 26. Unto you first God, having raised up his Son Jesus, sent him to bless you, in turning away every one of you from his iniquities. (Acts 3:11–26)

About five thousand men were saved after this sermon. "Howbeit many of them which heard the word believed; and the number of the men was about five thousand" (Acts 4:4).

3. Paul – from agreeing to Stephen's death to understanding and preaching the history himself.

A young man was present during the stoning of Stephen. "And cast him out of the city, and stoned him: and the witnesses laid down their clothes at a young man's feet, whose name was Saul" (Acts 7:58). After his consenting to Stephen's death, Saul made havoc of the church. He got special permission to go to Damascus to arrest the believers, but on the way, Jesus called him. Saul was saved, his name was changed to Paul, and he became a preacher of God's Word. (Read Acts 9:1–22 to remember Saul's conversion, at which time he was then called Paul.)

Paul preached Old Testament history in Romans 4.

A letter he sent back to the church at Corinth contained the following:

> 1. Moreover, brethren, I would not that ye should be ignorant, how that all our fathers were under the cloud, and all passed through the sea; 2. And were all baptized unto Moses in the cloud and in the sea; 3. And did all eat the same spiritual meat; 4. And did all drink the same spiritual drink: for they drank of that spiritual Rock that followed them: and that Rock was Christ. 5. But with many of them God was not well pleased: for they were overthrown in the wilderness. 6. Now these things were our examples, to the intent we should not lust after evil things, as they also lusted. 7. Neither be ye idolaters,

as were some of them; as it is written, The people sat down to eat and drink, and rose up to play. 8. Neither let us commit fornication, as some of them committed, and fell in one day three and twenty thousand. 9. Neither let us tempt Christ, as some of them also tempted, and were destroyed of serpents. 10. Neither murmur ye, as some of them also murmured, and were destroyed of the destroyer. 11. Now all these things happened unto them for ensamples: and they are written for our admonition, upon whom the ends of the world are come. 12. Wherefore let him that thinketh he standeth take heed lest he fall. (1 Corinthians 10:1–12)

As you have read, Paul also preached the history he had been taught from the time he was a child—history he did not fully *understand* until he received Jesus into his heart and life. He then realized that all of these things had happened for our examples. He proceeded to record their relevance for us to read and understand today. We need to remember this history (and live like we remember it), or we will fall.

NOTE The purpose of this Bible study is that each person who participates will realize that the Bible is more than a collection of stories. These were real events in real peoples' lives that fit together, like a puzzle, to form a definite picture that reveals God's Son, Jesus.

5. After Stephen challenged them, what did they do in Acts 7:54–60?

_____

_____

_____ What happened to Stephen

when he preached Jesus? (Acts 7:59) _____

_____

_____

6. What did Paul later write about the events of the Old Testament?
(1 Corinthians 10:11) _____

_____

THIRTY-NINE OLD TESTAMENT BOOKS: FIVE DIVISIONS

LESSON 4

Key Verse

This book of the law shall not depart out of thy mouth; but thou shalt meditate therein day and night, that thou mayest observe to do according to all that is written therein . . .

— JOSHUA 1:8

Key Verse Thought: (Look back at the poster of Old Testament bookshelf on page 15.) *Meditate* means "to dwell on any thing in thought; to contemplate; to study; to turn or revolve any subject in the mind."

Today, we will begin a study on how the Bible fits together. We will *meditate* on this for the next few weeks. By learning how God's Word fits together, it will be much easier for us to "observe to do according to all that is written therein."

Emphasis: Learn and become familiar with the five divisions of the thirty-nine Old Testament books.

Lesson Summary: Carefully look over the "Old Testament Overview." Become familiar with the basic divisions as you prepare to study them. This lesson will begin the learning process on how the Bible is divided into sections. These divisions will help us understand how the Bible fits together. It also will make it easier to find your favorite Bible stories and verses and help you to become a better Christian. We will understand how simply the Bible is laid out for us to see how it fits together. This cannot be learned in one lesson. This is just an overview of what we will learn in the weeks to come.

As we saw in the last lesson, the history in the Bible is very important. Today we will focus on the different divisions and how the Old Testament is laid out. This will help us understand the continuity of the scripture.

Suggested Bible Reading to Prepare for This Lesson

- ⊘ Monday: **Nehemiah 8**
- ⊘ Tuesday: **Deuteronomy 8**
- ⊘ Wednesday: **Job 1, 2**
- ⊘ Thursday: **Psalm 1**
- ⊘ Friday: **Nehemiah 9**
- ⊘ Saturday: **Luke 11**

Thirty-Nine Old Testament Books: Five Divisions

1 **Law (Pentateuch)—Five**

- Genesis–Deuteronomy
- Penned by Moses
- Five pre-Canaan history books

2 **Historical Books—Twelve**

- Joshua to Esther
- Joshua to 2 Chronicles: reveal history while Canaan is occupied (nine occupied)
- Ezra to Esther: reveal history after expulsion from Canaan (three post-exile)

3 **Personal Books—Five**

- Job to Song of Solomon
- Individual and experiential books
- Deal with problems of the individual heart and written as poems

4   Major Prophets—Five

- Isaiah to Daniel—prophetic
- Not only books of prophecy but Messiah foretold
- Isaiah and Jeremiah—pre-exile
- Lamentations and Ezekiel: intermediate; begin in homeland and are carried captive
- Daniel—exile

5   Minor Prophets—Twelve

- Hosea to Malachi—prophetic
- Hosea to Zephaniah (nine pre-exile)
- Haggai to Malachi (three post-exile)

What do you know?

1. **Law** — God created the world; Noah's ark; and Moses and the Ten Commandments are all found here.
2. **History** — Remember that David and Goliath happened here.
3. **Personal** — Learn that many of the Jews' songs were recorded here; remember the Twenty-Third Psalm or about Job.
4. **Major Prophets** — Remember Daniel and/or his three friends (Shadrach, Meshach, and Abednego).
5. **Minor Prophets** — Remember Jonah.

1. Law (Pentateuch)—Five

The word Pentateuch means "five books." Genesis, Exodus, Leviticus, Numbers, and Deuteronomy, the first five books of the Old Testament, are also referred to as "the Law." Moses recorded these books. Within these books, we find the first 2,500 years of history.

We see sin enter into the world, causing separation from God. We find God actively involved in men's lives.

See if you (or your students) can recall any events that fall within this group.

2. Historical Books—Twelve

The next twelve books pick up the history of the Israelites where it ended at the brink of the Promised Land (Israel, no longer called Canaan land) in Deuteronomy, completing the books of history: Joshua, Judges, Ruth, 1 Samuel, 2 Samuel, 1 Kings, 2 Kings, 1 Chronicles, 2 Chronicles, Ezra, Nehemiah, and Esther. The first nine record the history while the Jews occupy Israel. The last three reveal the period after they are carried away captive and then return to Israel.

> Twelve books that pick up the history of the Israelites where it ended at the brink of the Promise Land.

Within, we find the occupation and conquering of the Promised Land (Joshua) to the time of the judges (when the people turned from God, and they were then "judged"—Judges, Ruth). We then find the people rejecting God as their King, instead desiring an earthly king, a monarchy. From there the kingdom is divided and begins to decline, and they are carried captive to other lands (1 and 2 Samuel; 1 and 2 Kings; 1 and 2 Chronicles). Finally, the remnant (those who had been carried away captive) returns to the Promised Land, which is called Israel (Ezra, Nehemiah, Esther).

See if you (or your students) can recall any events that fall within this group.

3. Personal Books—Five

We call the following five books the Personal Books: Job, Psalms, Proverbs, Ecclesiastes, and Song of Solomon. They are books written as poems. They each deal with individuals' experiences with God and are very personal. They mainly deal with individuals' heart issues as they seek to know and better understand God.

> **The Personal Books are books written as poems.**

See if you (or your students) can recall any events that fall within this group.

4. Major Prophets—Five

The Major Prophets are the next five books: Isaiah, Jeremiah, Lamentations, Ezekiel, and Daniel.

Isaiah and Jeremiah were both prophets to the nation Israel before they were carried into captivity. Lamentations is a poem that reveals the horrors of seeing the city of Jerusalem and the temple of God destroyed after a terrible siege against the city. Ezekiel begins in Israel and ends in captivity in Babylon. Daniel was a prophet to the people after they were expelled from the Promised Land. Lamentations falls in the center of these five books, helping us see this division in history.

Another important thing to notice: Isaiah, Jeremiah, Ezekiel, and Daniel all contain specific prophecies concerning the coming Messiah. (We will research this later.)

See if you (or your students) can recall any events that fall within this group.

Daniel was a prophet to the people after they were expelled from the Promised Land.

The Five Books of the Law:
Genesis to Deuteronomy

1 ## Genesis

- The book of beginnings and revealing the sovereignty of God
- Four main events: the creation, the fall, the flood, the Tower of Babel
- Four main people: Abraham, Isaac, Jacob, Joseph

2 ## Exodus

- Ten plagues leading to the release of God's people from bondage in Egypt
- Reveals the importance of redemption by blood
- The Law is given: Ten Commandments
- Tabernacle described in detail

3 ## Leviticus

- God speaks from the tabernacle when it is completed
- God establishes offerings, the priesthood, a clean lifestyle, and the different feasts

- Teaches God's people to live a sanctified life (life set apart for a special purpose)
- Blessings of obedience and penalties for disobedience

4 Numbers

- Numbering and organization of the people
- A listing of the duties of the Levites and murmurings of the people
- Spies sent, rebellion of the people, discipline, and wanderings; ends with a second numbering of the people
- Joshua introduced as successor to Moses

5 Deuteronomy

- Looking back
- End of wanderings; preparing to resume the journey
- A second giving of the Law
- Joshua appointed new leader; Moses's death

1. Genesis

Genesis begins with the creation of all that is in existence. It records the ruin of man through sin (separation from God). Genesis also reveals the sovereignty of God, first in creation and then in the choosing of Abraham and his descendants in a covenant relationship. The word sovereignty means "(1) supreme in power; possessing supreme dominion; as a sovereign ruler of the universe; (2) supreme; superior to all others; chief."

God is the sovereign God of all who love and obey Him.

Four Main Events take place:
- The Creation — Genesis 1–2
- The Fall — Genesis 3–4
- The Flood — Genesis 6–9
- The Tower of Babel — Genesis 10–11

Think about these events briefly to remember them.

Genesis deals with Four People:
- Abraham — Genesis 12–23
- Isaac — Genesis 24–27
- Jacob — Genesis 27–35
- Joseph — Genesis 37–50

What can you remember about each of these characters? Try to grasp the important details to help you remember each character and his relation with the others. (We will go into much greater detail in future lessons. This is just to help you to understand the basics of the relationship and recognize in which book the events take place.)

2. Exodus

The word Exodus means "the way out" or "outgoing." The second book of the Old Testament reveals the redemption of God's people through the blood of a lamb.

Between Genesis and Exodus, God's people grew into a nation numbering around two to three million people. At least four hundred years had passed since they entered into Egypt. At the culmination of the ten plagues, we see the Israelites (those whose door posts were covered by the blood of a lamb) spared from the death angel and the mighty deliverance of God's people from a land of bondage (Egypt). The power of God was revealed through this time of Exodus.

Moses Given the Law on Mt. Sinai.

God spoke from the top of Mount Sinai, and it was there the Law was given (beginning with the Ten Commandments; Genesis 19–20). The Israelites were taught that obedience to God is necessary. They could not be a redeemed, set-apart people unless they obeyed God's commands.

Much of Exodus is dedicated to describing the tabernacle. God was very specific in the details. (We will see that detail about the tabernacle in future lessons.)

The book of Exodus ends with the tabernacle completed to God's specifications and the cloud covering the tent, filling the tabernacle with the glory of the Lord.

3. Leviticus

Once the tabernacle was completed, God spoke to Moses from there instead of Mount Sinai. Now that they were free from the land of bondage, the people needed to know how to live as a sanctified people.

God instituted the following:
- The offerings—Leviticus 1–7
- The priesthood—Leviticus 8–10; 12– 22
- A clean lifestyle—Leviticus 11–20
- The different feasts—Leviticus 23

God spoke to Moses from there instead of Mount Sinai.

Through these many things, the people were to learn how to live as a people wholly given to God in every aspect of their lives.

Leviticus shows the ability to have fellowship with God when we come to Him as a sanctified people (because He is a holy God, and we are a sinful people).

The book of Leviticus ends with the blessings of obedience, the penalties for disobedience, and with the importance of keeping vows to God. A warning is given to always keep our promises to God. (Only about a month's time passes during the book of Leviticus.)

4. Numbers

The name Numbers comes from a numbering of the people at the beginning of the book and then again at the end. These were two different groups of people:

- The old generation —Numbers 1–14
- A new generation —Numbers 21–36

When the twelve spies were sent into the land promised to Abraham, only Joshua and Caleb brought back a good report, claiming God would allow them to conquer the land. When the Israelites disobeyed God's command to cross over into the Promised Land, they were disciplined. The old generation would die and not enter into the Promised Land because they refused to obey God's command. Joshua and Caleb were the only ones to escape God's discipline (wandering in the wilderness for forty years; Numbers 15–20).

Moses and the Messengers from Canaan, painting by Giovanni Lanfranco, 1624.

Within Numbers we also find another listing of the Levites' duties, a murmuring of the people (in which they also are disciplined), and the death of Aaron.

Other stories of interest within Numbers are as follows:

- Miriam's leprosy—Numbers 12
- Korah's rebellion—Numbers 16
- Budding of Aaron's rod—Numbers 17
- Water from the rock—Numbers 20
- Fiery serpents—Numbers 21
- Balaam's donkey—Numbers 22

Fewer than forty years elapse during the book of Numbers. In that time, we see God guiding, providing, and protecting His people until they reach the Promised Land. As they prepared to enter, Joshua was introduced as the successor to Moses (Numbers 27:15–23).

Moses striking the rock.

5. Deuteronomy

Deuteronomy begins as a book looking back to what God had done for His people (Deuteronomy 1–11). The rest of the book looks forward (Deuteronomy 12–34). The entire book shows the faithfulness of God and reveals that God loves His people. "And because he loved thy fathers, therefore he chose their seed after them, and brought thee out in his sight with his mighty power out of Egypt" (Deuteronomy 4:37). "7. The LORD did not set his love upon you, nor choose you, because ye were more in number than any people; for ye were the fewest of all people: 8. But because the LORD loved you, and because he would keep the oath which he had sworn unto your fathers, hath the LORD brought you out with a mighty hand, and redeemed you out of the house of bondmen, from the hand of Pharaoh king of Egypt" (Deuteronomy 7:7–8).

Moses Pleading with Israel.

All of Israel gathered together. Moses warned the people not to forget the words of God's Law. Moses laid out before the people the blessings for following God's Law. He then warned them of the curse of God if they failed to obey. Deuteronomy reminds us of the Law, and the people are brought to the brink of the Promised Land, ready to continue.

Joshua is appointed the new leader (Deuteronomy 31), and Moses dies (Deuteronomy 34).

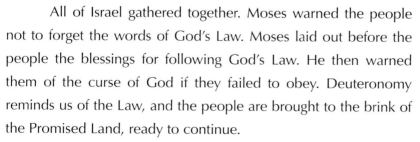

A Deeper Path:

Observe the things God is doing in your life. If you will only look, you will recognize that God is providing for and blessing you—but only if you are walking according to His commands. If not, you will see God's chastisement on your life. Just as breaking society's rules leads to punishment, you must become aware of God's punishment upon your life when you disobey God's commands (laws).

Reinforcement:

Continue memorizing the books of the Old Testament. Also be encouraged to make a concerted effort to obey God's Word.

Closing:

It would be good to close with a short prayer reinforcing today's lesson. Always include any prayer requests you may have. *Today, pray that we will understand not only the importance of God's Law but the importance of obeying God and His Word.*

LESSON 5

The Five Books of the Law: Genesis to Deuteronomy

Choose the correct book to fill in the blank:

Genesis, Exodus, Leviticus, Numbers, or Deuteronomy.

1. _____ A listing of the Levites' duties

Spies sent into Canaan

Begins and ends with a numbering

2. _____ Teaches to live a sanctified life

Blessings of obedience

God establishes the priesthood

3. _____ End of wanderings

A second giving of the law

Moses dies

4. _____ Tells of the flood

Tells of Abraham

Book of beginnings

5. _____ The Law is given
Tabernacle described in detail
Ten plagues leading to release
from Egypt

6. What does the word Pentateuch mean? _____
_____

7. What are the first five books of the Old Testament also called?
_____

TWELVE HISTORICAL BOOKS:
JOSHUA TO ESTHER

Key Verse

Remember therefore how thou hast received and heard, and hold fast, and repent

— REVELATION 3:3A

Key Verse Thought: What do you remember about anything we have been studying? Generate some discussion (if you are in a group), and then emphasize that we are studying these things to help us remember. Remember is the key word. If we don't remember and hold fast to what we learn from God's Word, we will never grow in Christ. The more we learn about God's Word, the more we will want to be like Him.

Emphasis: One importance of studying the history is to remember God's plan for His people. As we remember and hold fast to what we learn from God's Word, we will recognize God's plan for our lives. Remember what God's Word says.

Lesson Summary: Today we will study an overview of the twelve Historical Books. We have already discussed the importance of learning the history in the Bible. By learning it, we will understand the significance of why things happened. God had a plan, which is hard to understand unless you learn the Old Testament history. While it was happening, men didn't fully understand what that plan was, but through faith, they believed. The more we learn, the more pieces of the puzzle we can fit together. Each piece helps us become better students of God's Word, which helps us become better Christians.

This study ends the time frame of the Old Testament.

Suggested Bible Reading to Prepare for This Lesson

- ⊘ Monday: **Joshua 5**
- ⊘ Tuesday: **Judges 1–2**
- ⊘ Wednesday: **Ruth 4**
- ⊘ Thursday: **1 Samuel 8**
- ⊘ Friday: **2 Samuel 22**
- ⊘ Saturday: **Nehemiah 2**

Twelve Historical Books:
Joshua to Esther

1 **A Nation Ruled by God**

- Joshua
- Judges
- Ruth

2 **A Nation Ruled by Kings**

- 1 and 2 Samuel
- 1 and 2 Kings
- 1 and 2 Chronicles

3 **The Nation Restored to Their Land**

- Ezra
- Nehemiah
- Esther

Notice: These complete the seventeen total History books: Genesis to Esther. Three things are necessary to be a nation: people, land mass, and religion.

THE BIBLICAL PATH OF LIFE

2. A Nation Ruled by Kings

1 and 2 Samuel

First and Second Samuel reveal the lives of four main characters:

- Eli
- Samuel
- Saul
- David

Death of Saul.

The office of the priest was in a very low period. Eli and his sons were wicked men. Samuel was not only a good priest but a prophet of God. Saul became the first king of Israel but the kingdom was removed from him and his family forever because of his disobedience to God's words. "For rebellion is as the sin of witchcraft, and stubbornness is as iniquity and idolatry. Because thou hast rejected the word of the LORD, he hath also rejected thee from being king" (1 Samuel 15:23). The kingdom was then given to David and his descendants. "12. And when thy days be fulfilled, and thou shalt sleep with thy fathers, I will set up thy seed after thee, which shall proceed out of thy bowels, and I will establish his kingdom. ... 16. And thine house and thy kingdom shall be established for ever before thee: thy throne shall be established for ever" (2 Samuel 7:12, 16). This was not only a promise of his son, Solomon, who became the next king, but a promise that God's Son, Jesus, would one day be King of Kings.

1 and 2 Kings

The books of 1 and 2 Kings begin with King David's death and with his son, Solomon, taking the throne. One special thing to note is that much of the prophets' ministries take place during this time frame. (We will deal with this more specifically when we get to the books of the prophets.) During this time in Israel's history, we learn of the nation's decline from one of the greatest kingdoms ever to a completely nonexistent kingdom. When King Solomon turned his heart from God to idols, God divided the kingdom—but not until after King Solomon's death.

> The kingdom was divided as follows:
> - The Northern Kingdom, Israel
> - The Southern Kingdom, Judah

Israel (the Northern Kingdom) never had a good king. Judah (the Southern Kingdom) had a few. Mostly, God's people turned from worshipping God to worshipping idols. Despite the prophets' warnings, the people refused to turn back to God. God allowed both kingdoms to be taken captive. Israel was taken captive by Assyria, and later, Judah was taken captive by Babylon. Both places were made desolate, and the temple of God was destroyed.

1 and 2 Chronicles

The books of 1 and 2 Chronicles reveal the kingdom history from the priests' perspective (a spiritual point of view), whereas the books of Kings were written from the prophets' perspectives (a moral point of view.) These books help us understand the spiritual and moral reasons for the ultimate downfall of the nation Israel.

3. The Nation Restored to Their Land

Ezra

The book of Ezra shows us the beginning stages of the return of the people back to the land of Israel. The return of God's people took place in three stages. The first two are found in Ezra and the third in Nehemiah.

The first two stages of the return of God's people are as follows:

- The first return of people was led by Zerubbabel (Ezra 1–6, in which about eighty years pass). They had to overcome many obstacles. Their first act was to rebuild the altar. They then began working on the temple. Because of opposition, the building was stopped. Fifteen years passed before they completed the building of the temple.
- The second return of the remnant was led by Ezra (Ezra 7–10). About fifty-eight years divides these two returns. Ezra was a scribe and taught the people the Word of God to bring about very important reforms. He emphasized that they were to be a separate people. He encouraged them to separate themselves from the other people of the land.

Nehemiah

The book of Nehemiah is named for the man who was the cupbearer to the king Artaxerxes (in Persia). He received word that his beloved homeland lay in ruins; the walls were broken down, and the city gates were burned. Nehemiah had a burden for his people, and he took that burden to God. He prayed. God answered his prayer by allowing him to go to the city of Jerusalem and lead the people in rebuilding the walls and gates (about twelve years after Ezra led a remnant home). In spite of much opposition (they had to build with a sword in one hand), they completed the work in about seven weeks. The people were led to a time where the Word of God was read, the people repented, and they worshiped God (Nehemiah 8–9). In Nehemiah, we find the final stage of the return of God's people.

Esther

Esther is the only other book in the Bible to be named after a woman (Ruth being the first). The events in the book of Esther took place in history between the books of Ezra and Nehemiah. It dealt with the people who remained in the land of captivity instead of returning to Israel. In this book, God intervenes in history, using Esther (the Jewish young lady who became queen) and her cousin Mordecai to deliver His people from extermination. When faced with certain death because she was a Jew, the essence of the book is revealed in Esther's understanding of God's sovereignty. "Go, gather together all the Jews that are present in Shushan, and fast ye for me, and neither eat nor drink three days, night or day: I also and my maidens will fast likewise; and so will I go in unto the king, which is not according to the law: and if I perish, I perish" (Esther 4:16). She trusted that God knew what was happening and that He was in control. She allowed God to use her to deliver His people.

Esther accuses Haman.

Reinforcement:

Remember a specific time when you disobeyed God's commands. Was there any punishment? Did you recognize the break in fellowship with God? Do you remember what happened when the Israelites disobeyed and turned from God? (They were taken from their land.)

Reemphasize the importance of remembering this history we are studying. Obviously, it is too much to grasp all at once. This first quarter's lessons are only to whet one's appetite to want to learn more about God's Word. For now, we want to focus on the basics of the order of the Bible and understand how it fits together.

Closing:

It would be good to close with a short prayer reinforcing today's lesson. Always include any prayer requests you may have. *Pray for God to help us remember what God's Word says and understand how it fits together, much like pieces of a puzzle. Pray we will put our minds to remembrance of the things we learn.*

LESSON 6

Twelve Historical Books: Joshua to Esther

Complete the following:

1. What are the first five books of the Old Testament? _____

_____

_____

_____ These books are also considered historical books.

2. What three books tell of a nation supposed to be ruled by God?

_____

_____

3. What six books tell of a nation ruled by kings? _____

_____

_____

4. What three books tell of a nation restored to their land?_____

_____

_____

FIVE PERSONAL BOOKS:
JOB TO SONG OF SOLOMON

Key Verse

I have heard of thee by the hearing of the ear: but now mine eye seeth thee...

— JOB 42:5

Key Verse Thought: Read today's key verse. Has anyone ever "heard" God? Has anyone seen God? (Moses saw the back of God as God passed by; that's all we know of.) What does it really mean when people say they've "seen" God? (Understand that they have seen God move in their lives through events.) Today we will look at some men in the Bible who wanted to communicate with God, to know Him better. Each book is written as poems, and some are songs.

Emphasis: Recognize that "seeing" God refers to our seeing God move in our lives through events.

Lesson Summary: We will look at some men in the Bible who wanted to communicate with God and wanted to know Him better. Their words collectively are the five Personal Books, which are called such because they deal very personally with man. Each book was written as a poem, and each book deals with a different individual's experience with God. Become familiar with all five books. They are as follows:

- Job
- The men who wrote Psalms (David, Moses, and Asaph, who led the music)
- King Solomon, when he recorded wise words in Proverbs; when he wrote about the vanity of life apart from God in Ecclesiastes, and when he wrote of the beauty of a perfect love in marriage in Song of Solomon.

These books mainly deal with the individual's heart issues as he seeks to know and understand God better. We often set some these poems to music and sing them.

Suggested Bible Reading to Prepare for This Lesson

⊘	Monday:	**Job 1**
⊘	Tuesday:	**Job 42**
⊘	Wednesday:	**Psalm 23, 118**
⊘	Thursday:	**Proverbs 1–3**
⊘	Friday:	**Ecclesiastes 10–12**
⊘	Saturday:	**Song of Solomon 2**

Personal Books:
Job to Song of Solomon

1 ## Job

- Satan presents himself before God's throne (Job 1:6–12).
- God allows Satan to attack Job.
- Job grows in his knowledge of who God is.

2 ## Psalms

- This book is known as the Israelites' songbook.
- They are not only songs but prayers from the heart.

3 ## Proverbs

- The book of wisdom.
- Wise words to apply to our lives

4 ## Ecclesiastes

- This book was written by King Solomon, recording the vanity of life.

- Solomon found man could not make sense of life apart from God.

5 Song of Solomon

- This was written as a love song from King Solomon to a young maiden.
- This book is a picture of Christ's love for the church.

Godly songs help us remember God's Word and to praise God often!

- King David wrote almost half of the Psalms
- King David's son, King Solomon, wrote three of the books (Proverbs, Ecclesiastes, and Song of Solomon).

1. Job

Job receiving the messangers.

Job opens with a behind-the-scenes event that Job never knew about (a very important fact for us to consider!). We read of Satan presenting himself before God's throne. God (who knows all) asked if he had set his heart upon God's servant, Job. The rest of the book records the events that transpired. It's most important to note that through the events that took place in this book, a man known as a "perfect and upright man, one that feareth God, and escheweth [turns away from] evil" (Job 1:8), Job still grew in his knowledge of God. "5. I have heard of thee by the hearing of the ear: but now mine eye seeth thee. 6. Wherefore I abhor myself, and repent in dust and ashes" (Job 42:5–6).

Many believe the book of Job took place about the same time as Abraham, but most agree that this is the oldest book written.

Take time to read more of the book of Job to see in greater detail the events that transpired in his life. Understand that even though Job is recorded as a "perfect and upright man," he still grew in his knowledge of God. Even though many people may have been in Sunday School most of their lives, and think they know enough, most people can still grow in their knowledge of God's Word. No one should ever lose that desire to learn more about God. Job didn't!

2. Psalms

David is often credited as the author of Psalms. Although he probably wrote almost half of them (about seventy-three), there were other authors, known and unknown. The book is divided into five different books, each ending with its own doxology (a hymn of praise to God). They parallel the first five books in the Bible, the books of Moses. (We will look at the specifics later as we study Psalms.)

Many of the Psalms were written when different men approached God in prayer because of their circumstances. You can see instances of great sorrow, admitted sin, repentance, hope and trust in God, faith, and a great love for God. Some were written in praise and adoration of who God is versus who man is. Many of these hymns are rich in Israel's history. If we know the history, we will better understand the circumstances surrounding many of these songs.

Psalms Book ancient page cover.

3. Proverbs

Proverbs is known as a great source of wisdom. The wisest man, Solomon, whose wisdom was a gift from God (1 Kings 3:12), wrote many of these words. "7. The fear of the LORD is the beginning of knowledge: but fools despise wisdom and instruction. 8. My son, hear the instruction of thy father, and forsake not the law of thy mother" (Proverbs 1:7–8). These words of wisdom were written to help us live our daily lives wisely. Often it compares the wise with the fool. The precepts within are very practical. Much good will come to those who not only memorize these pearls of wisdom, but for those who apply these truths to their lives.

Solomon writing Proverbs

4. Ecclesiastes

Ecclesiastes was written by King Solomon, the man who had it all—wealth, fame, a rich heritage, a personal relationship with God, and wisdom beyond measure. Yet with all of that, he found that all of life was "vanity and vexation." (*Vanity* refers to any thing that is futile, or worthless; *vexation* refers to something that disturbs or annoys; to trouble seriously.) He repeats the phrase "vanity and vexation" seven times in Ecclesiastes. "I have seen all the works that are done under the sun; and, behold, all is vanity and vexation of spirit" (Ecclesiastes 1:14). *Vanity*, here, means emptiness, something unsatisfactory. Solomon had not learned how to restrain his desires, and that was the cause of all of his "vanity and vexation." Even with all of his wisdom, Solomon did not have all the answers of life. He wrote this book from a worldly man's point of view. He tried to make sense of life apart from God, yet he couldn't. His final conclusion? "13. Let us hear the conclusion of the whole matter: Fear God, and keep his commandments: for this is the whole duty of man. 14. For God shall bring every work into judgment, with every secret thing, whether it be good, or whether it be evil" (Ecclesiastes 12:13–14).

The iron worker and King Solomon.

LESSON 7

Five Personal Books:
Job to Song of Solomon

Choose the correct book to fill in the blank:

Job, Psalms, Proverbs, Ecclesiastes, Song of Solomon.

1. _____ Man can't make sense of life apart
   from God
   Records the vanity of life
   Written by King Solomon

2. _____ Written as a love song
   Picture of Christ's love
   for the church
   From King Solomon to
   a young maiden

3. _____ Grows in his knowledge
   of who God is God allowed
   Satan to attack him
   Satan presented himself
   before God's throne

4. _____ Wise things to apply to our lives

Book of wisdom

Mostly written by King Solomon

5. _____ Prayers from the heart

Many written by King David

Known as the Israelites' songbook

6. Why are these books called the personal books?_____

_____

_____

7. In what form were these books originally written?_____

_____

_____

SEVENTEEN PROPHETIC BOOKS: ISAIAH TO MALACHI

LESSON 8

Key Verse

That it might be fulfilled which was spoken by the prophet, saying, I will open my mouth in parables; I will utter things which have been kept secret from the foundation of the world.

— MATTHEW 13:35

Key Verse Thought: Have you ever been told a secret? Did you want to keep it a secret or tell someone else? Secrets are hard to keep, yet the most important "secret" ever is not shared nearly enough. God had secrets, and He told many of them to His people. We can know those secrets today if we will just read His Word.

Read the key verse again to understand it. The prophets revealed secrets that had been "kept secret from the foundation of the world." Today we will look at the prophets and become familiar with who they are. In the future, we will study them deeper.

NOTE God wants us to understand the mysteries or secrets of the Old Testament. He wants us to realize that it all centered on the coming of Jesus, God's Son. "25. Now to him that is of power to stablish you according to my gospel, and the preaching of Jesus Christ, according to the revelation of the mystery, which was kept secret since the world began, 26. But now is made manifest, and by the scriptures of the prophets, according to the commandment of the everlasting God, made known to all nations for the obedience of faith" (Romans 16:25–26).

Emphasis: Recognize that God wants us to understand the mysteries or secrets of the Old Testament, for they are centered on reminding us of the coming of Jesus, God's Son.

Lesson Summary: When God's people were in sin and rebellion, God sent a prophet to speak His words to the people. The word prophet means "one who speaks in place of another." Often, they would say, "Thus saith the Lord." Many times they brought a message to the people, warning of the chastisement that was to come if the people did not repent and turn their hearts back to God and His commands. Their primary job was not to foretell the future, although at times they did. Prophets were usually unpopular in the land.

Today's lesson is an introduction to the prophets. If you have students, help them become familiar with the names and in which books of the Bible the events of the prophets' lives are found (when they prophesied). Understand that just because the books of the prophets are found at the end of the Old Testament, this is not necessarily the time frame in history that they occurred. We end with an event in the New Testament that helps understand why we need to know the prophets.

Suggested Bible Reading to Prepare for This Lesson

- ⊘ Monday: **Isaiah 53**
- ⊘ Tuesday: **Daniel 9**
- ⊘ Wednesday: **Jeremiah 9**
- ⊘ Thursday: **Ezekiel 24**
- ⊘ Friday: **Malachi 3**
- ⊘ Saturday: **Luke 16**

Seventeen Prophetic Books:
Isaiah to Malachi

1 **Five Major Prophets**

- Isaiah to Daniel—prophetic
- Not only books of prophecy but Messiah foretold
- Isaiah and Jeremiah—pre-exile
- Lamentations and Ezekiel—intermediate; began in homeland and are carried captive
- Daniel—exile

2 **Nine Minor Prophets—Pre-exile**

- Prophets to Judah: Joel, Micah, Habakkuk, Zephaniah
- Prophets to Israel: Hosea, Amos
- Prophets to other lands: Obadiah (Edom), Jonah (Nineveh), Nahum (Assyria)

3 **Three Minor Prophets—Post-exile**

- All three prophesied to the returned remnant
- Haggai and Zechariah were contemporaries
- Haggai prophesied about Ezra 5–6; Zechariah began shortly thereafter
- Malachi prophesied about a century later

4 **The Rich Man and Lazarus**

- Luke 16:14–16, 19–31

1. Five Major Prophets

The Major Prophets are the next five books: Isaiah, Jeremiah, Lamentations, Ezekiel, and Daniel.

Prophets were called such because they were messengers of God, called by God to proclaim God's words to the people. God used many avenues to speak to these men: angels, dreams, visions, miracles, and even an audible voice. Their job was not to tell the future, although many times they did foretell future events. Primarily, they were to expose the sins of the people, revealing the need for repentance (turning a humble heart back to God). Prophets were to also remind the people of God's laws and that the people were to obey them. They warned of God's judgment on those who refused to obey. Most importantly, the prophets reminded the people that the Promised One (Jesus) would come. They gave many insights as to the timing, the place, and even the manner in which He would come.

Isaiah and *Jeremiah* were both prophets to the nation Israel before they were carried into captivity. Isaiah examined the sins of Judah. He spoke to the kings in their courts. He then pronounced the judgment of God on the nation (including the nations around). Isaiah is known as a prophet who foretold the Babylonian conquest and Jesus coming as our suffering Savior. By the time Jeremiah came, the people were deep in moral and even spiritual depravity. He declared the coming certain judgment for the people's sins but with the promise of restoration. Jeremiah is known as the Weeping Prophet; he foretold Jesus as the "Branch" of David.

Lamentations is a poem that reveals the horrors of seeing the city of Jerusalem and the temple of God destroyed after a terrible siege against the city. It falls in the center of these five books, helping us see this division in history. Lamentations is a poem by Jeremiah on the fall of Jerusalem. As Jeremiah was ending his prophecies in Jerusalem, Ezekiel was beginning his ministry among the exiles.

The vision of prophet Ezekiel.

Ezekiel begins in Israel and ends in captivity in Babylon (Ezekiel probably wrote Psalm 137), although his prophecies began after he was taken captive (Ezekiel 1:2–3). Ezekiel is known as the prophet who foretold of our shepherd King.

Daniel was a prophet to the people after they were expelled from the Promised Land. It contains many specific prophecies. Some have yet to be fulfilled. The first half of the book records many events in the lives of Daniel and his three friends as they remain faithful to God, even though they were taken from their homeland. They are mighty examples for us to remain a separate and faithful people, despite adverse circumstances. Daniel is known as the prophet who foretold that the Messiah would be "cut off."

Another important thing to notice is that Isaiah, Jeremiah, Ezekiel, and Daniel all contain *specific* prophecies concerning the coming Messiah. (We will research this later.)

2. Nine Minor Prophets: Pre-exile

The first nine minor prophets are included in the final division in the Old Testament: Hosea, Joel, Amos, Obadiah, Jonah, Micah, Nahum, Habakkuk, and Zephaniah. Once again we see an obvious division; these are pre-exile—before the people were expelled from Israel.

Joel told of the plague of locusts.

    Joel prophesied to Judah during the reign of Jehoash (Joash) that began in 2 Kings 12.

Micah was known as a prophet to both Israel and Judah, calling for people to "hear."

    Micah prophesied to Judah during the reign of Hezekiah that began in 2 Kings 18.

Habakkuk was known as the prophet who asked God why—and God answered.

    Habakkuk prophesied to Judah during the reign of Josiah that began in 2 Kings 22.

Zephaniah wrote of God's judgment and mercy.

    Zephaniah prophesied to Judah during the reign of Josiah that began in 2 Kings 22.

Hosea revealed the love of God in spite of spiritual adultery.

     Hosea prophesied to Israel during the reign of Uzziah (Azariah) that began in 2 Kings 15.

Amos was known as a prophet from the country.

     Amos prophesied to Israel during the reign of Jeroboam II that began in 2 Kings 14:16.

Obadiah was written as a warning to those who persecute Israelites.

     Obadiah prophesied to Edom and is considered one of the older books of prophecy.

Jonah was known as an unwilling or reluctant prophet.

     Jonah prophesied to Nineveh (in Assyria), about the time of 2 Kings 14.

Nahum was known as one who prophesied the destruction of Nineveh.

     Nahum prophesied to Assyria, about the time of 2 Kings 21.

Vision of Obadiah.

3. Three Minor Prophets: Post-exile

The last three books of prophecy (Haggai, Zechariah, and Malachi) are post-exile, after the people are carried away captive.

Haggai was known as a prophet who reminded the people that God comes first.

Haggai prophesied to the returning remnant during the leadership of Zerubbabel.

Zechariah encouraged the people to finish, as God wasn't finished with them yet.

Zechariah (who also was a priest) prophesied to the returning remnant during the leadership of Zerubbabel.

Malachi was known as the last call to return to God before a four-hundred-year silence.

Malachi, about a century after the return, was a last prophetic call, ending the Old Testament with a curse.

NOTE Remember that the Major Prophets are not more important than the Minor Prophets. They are called major and minor because of the volume of their content.

4. The Rich Man and Lazarus

Read Luke 16:14–16. After reading it, understand that the Pharisees were the religious leaders in the New Testament times. They had studied the Law and Prophets much as we are doing in this study. From the time they were children, they learned the importance of obeying God's Word. From outward appearances, it looked like they were living exactly as they were supposed to be living in God's Word, but Jesus knew their hearts. Just because they acted the right way and talked the right way did not mean their hearts were right. In these verses, Jesus is letting them know that their hearts were not right and that they were an "abomination in the sight of God." Abomination means "that which is detestable to God." Jesus told them that the Law and the Prophets (those we have been looking at) were until John (see Luke 16:16 and John the Baptist, who came to tell of the Lamb of God, who came to take away the sins of the world—Jesus; see John 1:29). Now they had Jesus, who was a fulfillment of the Law and the Prophets' words.

Jesus then proceeded to tell these Pharisees about the rich man and Lazarus. Read Luke 16:19–31. From all appearances, the rich man had everything this world had to offer. Lazarus, on the other hand, had absolutely nothing, but he believed in Jesus. We know because immediately when he died, he was in the bosom of Abraham. Remember Abraham, to whom God made a covenant (promise) centuries earlier? When the rich man died, he went to hell, a place of torment with flames (Luke 16:23–24). When the rich man understood what had happened, he wanted Lazarus to become alive again to go and warn his five brothers who were still alive but heading for hell, too. He understood it was too late for him, but he wanted to warn his brothers. "29. Abraham saith unto him, They have Moses and the prophets; let them hear them. 30. And he said, Nay, father Abraham: but if one went unto them from the dead, they will repent. 31. And he said unto him, If they hear not Moses and the prophets, neither will they be persuaded, though one rose from the dead" (Luke 16:29–31). All the rich man and his five brothers needed to hear had been said by Moses and the Prophets. His five brothers wouldn't believe Lazarus if he had risen from the dead, just as people today still refuse to believe Jesus, though he died on the cross to pay for their sins and rose from the dead to proclaim that fact to the world.

A Deeper Path:

You could go into much more detail about what hell is really like. (To read some verses on hell, see Matthew 13:42; Mark 9:43b-44; 2 Thessalonians 1:7–9; Revelation 20:10, 14–15.) Understand the plan of salvation clearly; remember the "Roman Road".

1. You first must recognize you are lost (having commited sin; disobedience to any of God's commands).

   Lostness: "For all have sinned, and come short of the glory of God" (Romans 3:23).

2. You must then understand the consequences, or penalty, for that sin (punishment or eternal life by Jesus).

   Penalty: "For the wages of sin is death; but the gift of God is eternal life through Jesus Christ our Lord." (Romans 6:23).

3. What is the price for this eternal life?

> **Price:** "But God commendeth his love toward us, in that, while we were yet sinners, Christ died for us" (Romans 5:8).

4. What response should be made?

> **Response:** "9. That if thou shalt confess with thy mouth the Lord Jesus, and shalt believe in thine heart that God hath raised him from the dead, thou shalt be saved. 10. For with the heart man believeth unto righteousness; and with the mouth confession is made unto salvation" (Romans 10:9–10).

5. What security of eternal life do I have if I ever commit another sin?

> **Security:** "38. For I am persuaded, that neither death, nor life, nor angels, nor principalities, nor powers, nor things present, nor things to come, 39. Nor height, nor depth, nor any other creature, shall be able to separate us from the love of God, which is in Christ Jesus our Lord" (Romans 8:38–39).

6. How do I live this New Life, free from sin?

> **New Life:** "1. I beseech you therefore, brethren, by the mercies of God, that ye present your bodies a living sacrifice, holy, acceptable unto God, which is your reasonable service. 2. And be not conformed to this world: but be ye transformed by the renewing of your mind, that ye may prove what is that good, and acceptable, and perfect, will of God" (Romans 12:1–2). Don't live like the world lives anymore. Read God's Word, and you will learn how to please God.

Reinforcement:

Consider what we learned today. The Bible is full of mysteries. With Jesus in our hearts and God's Word read daily, we can understand those mysteries. We don't need prophets today because we have the prophets' words written in the Bible. Our job is to know God's Word so we can share the message of Jesus to the world. The words recorded in the books of the Old Testament are very important. We study them to understand why we need Jesus and why we need to live a life pleasing to God (by obeying His commands). As we saw as Jesus told of the rich man and Lazarus, the Law and the Prophets had the words that could have saved his soul for eternity if he had only believed them. It's very important to understand that just because we act the right way and say the right things (as the Pharisees did), without Jesus in our hearts, it is never enough. As we learned today, many of the prophets' words were warnings to the people. Can you think of any words of warning to which we ourselves should listen? Are there any words of warning we need to share with our friends?

You might take time to make a list of lost friends or family to pray for. Make an effort to pray for these people often.

Closing:

It would be good to close with a short prayer reinforcing today's lesson. Always include any prayer requests you may have. *Today, pray for God to help us to want to know more "secrets" in the Bible. Also, pray to help us keep our hearts turned toward God so we can please Him. Also pray for God to help us to know for sure we belong to Him. Give us a burden for our lost friends and family (those who don't have Jesus in their hearts).*

Seventeen Prophetic Books:
Isaiah to Malachi

Complete the following:

1. List the five Major Prophets _____

_____

2. Which two of the five Major Prophets books spoke before the exile? _____

_____

3. Which of the five Major Prophets began in the homeland and was carried captive? _____

4. Which of the five Major Prophet books was during the exile?

_____

5. List the twelve Minor Prophets. _____

_____

_____

Answers:
1. Isaiah, Jeremiah, Lamentations, Ezekiel, Daniel; 2. Isaiah and Jeremiah; 3. Ezekiel; 4. Daniel; 5. Hosea, Joel, Amos, Obadiah, Jonah, Mica, Nahum, Habakkuk, Zephaniah, Haggai, Zechariah, Malachi;

6. List the nine Minor Prophets that were before the captivity. _____

_____

_____

_____

7. Who were the four prophets to Judah? _____

_____

8. Who were the two prophets to Israel? _____

_____

9. Who spoke to Edom? _____ Who spoke to Ninevah?
_____ Who spoke to Assyria? _____

10. List the three Minor Prophets who prophesied to the returned remnant from captivity. _____

_____

11. Who was the last prophet to speak?_____
About how much later did he speak?_____

12. After reading about the rich man and Lazarus, why is it important to know about the prophets? _____

Answers:
6. Hosea, Joel, Amos, Obadiah, Jonah, Micah, Nahum, Habakkuk, Zephaniah; **7.** Joel, Micah, Habakkuk, Zephaniah; **8.** Hosea and Amos; **9.** Obadiah; Jonah; Amos; **10.** Haggai, Zechariah, Malachi; **11.** Malachi; about a century; **12.** They tell about Jesus

FIVE MAJOR PROPHETS: ISAIAH TO DANIEL

Key Verse

Seek good, and not evil, that ye may live: and so the LORD, the God of hosts, shall be with you, as ye have spoken.

— AMOS 5:14

Key Verse Thought: After reading the key verse, understand the word seek means "to search." We must seek good things in this world, not evil. In our lesson today, we find that God's people had quit seeking good and were continually doing evil. Remember, God spoke to His people through prophets many years ago. God sent His prophets to tell the people to seek God and follow His commands.

Emphasis: Much of the prophets' message was to "seek good, and not evil." We must continue to seek good and learn to always obey God's commands.

Lesson Summary: If you think about it, the prophets had a fascinating role in history. God sent His prophets to tell the people to seek God and follow His commands. They were entrusted with God's Word to be delivered to the people. Exposing the sins of the people and revealing the need for repentance (turning a humble heart back to God) took much courage. Although it was a difficult task, we see faithful men accomplish what God asked of them. Even when the people refused to listen at the time, we see God working to fulfill His plan. As teachers, and students of the Bible, we should never be afraid to study the words written in the books of prophecy. Remember, the prophets also reminded the people that the Promised One (Jesus) would come. Take note: God knew and chose these men.

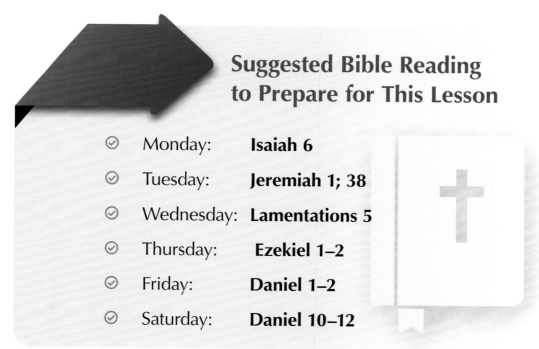

Suggested Bible Reading to Prepare for This Lesson

- ⊘ Monday: **Isaiah 6**
- ⊘ Tuesday: **Jeremiah 1; 38**
- ⊘ Wednesday: **Lamentations 5**
- ⊘ Thursday: **Ezekiel 1–2**
- ⊘ Friday: **Daniel 1–2**
- ⊘ Saturday: **Daniel 10–12**

Five Major Prophets:
Isaiah to Daniel

1 ## Isaiah
- Called in Isaiah 6
- Prophet to Judah; speaking to the kings in their courts
- Witnessed the carrying away of Israel (Northern Kingdom) into captivity

2 ## Jeremiah
- God knew Jeremiah would be a prophet before he was born
- Being both priest and prophet, he prophesied about one hundred years after Isaiah
- Preached coming judgment and witnessed it come to pass
- Saw five kings in Judah, with only one good king (Josiah)

3 ## Lamentations
- Poem depicting the destruction of Jerusalem and the captivity of God's people
- Written by Jeremiah

4 ## Ezekiel
- Called in Ezekiel 1:28–2:10
- Carried away captive and prophesied to the captives in a foreign land

5 Daniel

- Obeyed God rather than man
- Daniel 1–6 records Daniel and his three friends lived faithfully in foreign land
- The books of Daniel and Revelation go hand in hand to help us understand prophecies

Remember

We learned in our last lesson that prophets were called such because they were messengers of God, men whom God called to proclaim "the word of the Lord" to His people, the Israelites. The Gentile nations were usually only mentioned as either a source of conflict with the nation or for being blessed because of Israel. Primarily, the prophets were to expose the sins of the people, revealing the need for repentance and to remind the people to obey God's laws. The prophets, however, told of two very important events: the first and second coming of Jesus. They gave many insights as to the timing, the place, and even the manner in which He would come. Even when they could not fully understand everything they recorded in God's Word for us to read today, they were faithful to obey God and His commands.

1. Isaiah

Isaiah was called to be a prophet in the year King Uzziah died (Isaiah 6) and lived into the reign of Manasseh, one of the worst kings Judah had. He prophesied for about forty years. Tradition says that Manasseh had Isaiah "sawn asunder." Isaiah was a prophet to Judah before they were carried into captivity, but he saw Israel carried into captivity by Assyria.

Isaiah examines the sins of Judah, speaking to the kings in their courts.

Isaiah is often quoted in the New Testament. Jesus quoted from it often. Remember that the Ethiopian eunuch was reading the book of Isaiah when Phillip showed him how to be saved.

Isaiah is known as a prophet who foretold of the Babylonian conquest and Jesus's coming as our suffering Savior. Isaiah records many specific prophecies concerning the coming Messiah, more than any other book in the Old Testament. (We will study this later.)

NOTE

God called Isaiah. God asked who He could send; who would go? Isaiah answered God's call to go and tell (Isaiah 6:1–13). He obeyed when God called.

2. Jeremiah

Jeremiah lived about one hundred years after Isaiah. Jeremiah was both a priest and prophet. God knew Jeremiah would be a prophet before he was even born (Jeremiah 1:4–5). He saw five kings, with only one of them, King Josiah, being a godly king. Jeremiah preached during his reign (Jeremiah 2–12), during which time King Josiah began eliminating idolatry and cleaning out the temple. While repairing the temple, a copy of the Law was found. The king read the Law, which led to repentance and reformation.

Jeremiah prophesied the people would be held in captivity for seventy years (Jeremiah 25). This scripture encouraged and inspired Daniel who was held captive in Babylon (Daniel 9).

Jeremiah wrote the words of the Lord, but the evil king Jehoiakim cut it up with a penknife and threw it into a fire (Jeremiah 36).

Jeremiah was a prophet to Judah before they were carried into captivity. Tradition has it that Jeremiah was stoned to death.

Jeremiah is known as the Weeping Prophet and foretold Jesus as the "Branch" of David.

NOTE God knew Jeremiah before he was born. He knew Jeremiah would be a prophet for God (Jeremiah 1:4–10). He called, prepared, sent, and promised to be with Jeremiah. Jeremiah prophesied for over forty years. Remember that God never gives us anything to do that He won't help us complete, if we only will trust Him (as did Jeremiah and the other prophets).

3. Lamentations

Lamentations (written by Jeremiah) is a poem revealing the horrors of seeing the city of Jerusalem and the temple of God destroyed after a terrible siege against the city. It falls in the center of these five books, helping us see this division in history.

Lamentations clearly depicts sin, its consequences, and the need to return to God for His mercy.

Lamentations is a poem by Jeremiah on the fall of Jerusalem.

Lamentations of Jeremiah

4. Ezekiel

While Jeremiah was ending his prophecies in Jerusalem, Ezekiel was beginning his ministry among the exiles. He was called by God (Ezekiel 1:26–2:10). Ezekiel, also a priest and a prophet, began in Israel, was captured, and ended in captivity in Babylon. Psalm 137 was probably written by Ezekiel, although his prophecies began once he was taken captive (Ezekiel 1:2–3). Ezekiel was carried away to Babylon (during the second carrying away) by Nebuchadnezzar with the best of the Judean nobility. His ministry didn't begin until the fifth year after he arrived in Babylon. (At this time, Jerusalem was still standing.)

Later, Ezekiel had the task of telling the generation born in captivity about the sins that led to the people's exile. Note: Many of the children who heard him

The Prophet Ezekiel.

preach were the ones who later returned to Jerusalem after the seventy years of captivity. It is extremely important that we teach our children.

Points of Interest

- "They shall know that I am the Lord" appears about sixty-five times in the book of Ezekiel.
- "The son of man" is mentioned about forty-five times.
- "The glory of the Lord" is used about fifteen times.
- Prophecies tell of the impending fall of Jerusalem (Ezekiel 1–24).
- He saw the cloud of Shekinah glory slowly depart Jerusalem (Ezekiel 9–10).
- "Valley of Dry Bones" is mentioned in Ezekiel 37.

Ezekiel is known as the prophet who foretold of our shepherd King.

NOTE Ezekiel's call is found in Ezekiel 1:28–2:10. Solemn charge was given to him in Ezekiel 3:16–21.

5. Daniel

Daniel was a prophet to the people after they were expelled from the Promised Land. The first half of the book (Daniel 1–6) records many events in the lives of Daniel and his three friends as they remain faithful to God, even though they were taken from their homeland. They were young men of conviction. They were not afraid to stand and choose to obey God rather than man. They are mighty examples for us to remain a separate and faithful people, despite adverse circumstances.

Remember that Daniel was taken from his homeland. While he was in Babylon, he read the book of Jeremiah. He found something that encouraged him greatly. (Read Daniel 9:2.) He understood that the people would only be captive from their homeland for seventy years, and then they could return. He found a piece of the puzzle and understood what God was doing. We can do the same, if we will take the time to read God's Word daily.

Daniel contains many specific prophecies. Some have yet to be fulfilled. Revelation cannot be properly understood without understanding Daniel. A portion of every chapter of Daniel is referred to or quoted in all but two chapters in Revelation. Jesus referred to Daniel (the book and the man) many times.

Daniel is known as the prophet who foretold that the Messiah would be "cut off."

NOTE Daniel proved himself worthy to be used by God when he refused to obey the king and instead chose to obey God's commands.

Reinforcement:

Because only God knows all, we sometimes have trouble obeying when we don't understand. As we saw today, the prophets were faithful men who followed God, even when they didn't completely understand. Sometimes the prophet held only a piece of the future event. Remember the "pieces" we have been talking about? Remember Daniel when he read the book of Jeremiah? These prophets each held different pieces of information given to them by God. Now we can read the entirety and put those pieces together and see they all point to Jesus.

Closing:

It would be good to close with a short prayer reinforcing today's lesson. Always include any prayer requests you may have. *Today, pray, asking God to help us seek good and not evil so we can please Him. Ask God to show us where we fail so that we can correct our lives.*

LESSON 9

The Five Major Prophets:
Isaiah to Daniel

Complete the following:

1. List the five Major Prophets. _____
_____

2. Tell about Isaiah's call in Isaiah 6. _____
_____
_____

3. Which two prophets spoke to Judah before the captivity? _____
_____

4. Who saw five good kings in Judah, with only one of them being
a good king? _____
Who was the good king? _____

5. Who prophesied about one hundred years after Isaiah? _____
_____

6. Who wrote the book of Lamentations? _____
What was it about? _____
_____

7. Tell about the call of Ezekiel (Ezekiel 1:26– 2:10). _____

_____

_____

_____

8. What happened to Ezekiel, and what did he do? _____

_____

_____

9. Who chose to obey God rather than man? _____

_____

10. Who lived faithfully in a foreign land? _____

_____

_____

NINE PRE-EXILE MINOR PROPHETS: HOSEA TO ZEPHANIAH

LESSON 10

Key Verse

God, who at sundry times and in divers manners spake in time past unto the fathers by the prophets.

— HEBREWS 1:1

Key Verse Thought: Understand the key verse: "God, who at sundry times [refers to the incremental and progressive manner in which God disclosed Himself, up until the appearance of the Son. It was fragmentary, piece by piece, like pieces of a puzzle] and in divers manners [this word is used to qualify the manner in which divine revelation during the Old Testament time frame was given. It shows the diverse ways through which God disclosed His Word, such as dreams, visions, and angelic visitation] spake in time past unto the fathers by the prophets."

Today, we will learn about some men who God called for a special purpose. One of these disobeyed God. See what happened to him!

Emphasis: God revealed Himself to people through the ages in different ways at different times. He had an extra-special job for the prophets. God has an extra-special job for His people today as well—if we will only obey! Make your time on earth count for God; live for him daily. Allow God to use you. Respond when God calls. It may be a minor thing in your eyes that God asks of you but very important to the kingdom of God.

Lesson Summary: The first nine Minor Prophets are included in the final division in the Old Testament: Hosea, Joel, Amos,

Obadiah, Jonah, Micah, Nahum, Habakkuk, and Zephaniah. Once again we see there is an obvious division; these are pre-exile, before the people were expelled from Israel. Interestingly, we know very little about these prophets. Amos was a herdsman (Amos 7:14), Micah was from an obscure town twenty-five miles southwest of Jerusalem who preached to the poor and oppressed, and Zephaniah was a descendant of good King Hezekiah. They were just ordinary men who God chose to use.

Emphasize: Make your time on earth count for God. Live for Him daily. Allow God to use you.

First we will look at the prophets to Judah, then Israel, and finally the prophets to Gentile nations:

Suggested Bible Reading to Prepare for This Lesson

- Monday: **Hosea 1–3**
- Tuesday: **Joel 1–3**
- Wednesday: **Amos 1; Obadiah 1**
- Thursday: **Jonah 1–4**
- Friday: **Micah 1–2; Nahum 1**
- Saturday: **Obadiah 1**

Nine Pre-Exile Minor Prophets:
Hosea to Zephaniah

1 Prophets to Judah

- Joel
- Micah
- Habakkuk
- Zephaniah

2 Prophets to Israel

- Hosea
- Amos

3 Prophets to Other Lands

- Obadiah
- Jonah
- Nahum

1. Prophets to Judah

The book of Joel begins with, "The word of the Lord that came to Joel …" God spoke, and Joel relayed God's message to the people. After seeing a plague of locust, Joel warned of a coming invasion that he compared to that plague of locusts. Just as a plague of locusts completely destroys everything in its path, so the enemies of God would do to His people unless they repented of their sins against God. Joel prophesied to Judah during the reign of Jehoash (Joash) that began in 2 Kings 12.

Joel told of the plague of locusts.

The book of Micah begins with, "The word of the Lord that came to Micah …" He told of the coming judgment but also of the future blessing. He, too, calls the people to repentance and a right relationship with God. "He hath shewed thee, O man, what is good; and what doth the LORD require of thee, but to do justly, and to love mercy, and to walk humbly with thy God?" (Micah 6:8). Micah prophesied to Judah (although he often included Samaria) during the reign of Hezekiah that began in 2 Kings 18. We often remember Micah as the book that tells that the birth of Jesus will be in Bethlehem (Micah 5:2).

Micah is known as a prophet to both Israel and Judah, calling for people to "hear."

Habakkuk is a unique prophet in that he saw the condition of God's people, and it disturbed him greatly. He then asked God how long this condition would continue. He knew that God's people who were living in continual sin would be punished. God answered him. When Habakkuk didn't understand how God could use a sinful nation to discipline God's people, he went to God again for the answer. God answered him again. He learned that he must have faith in God. "… but the just shall live by his faith" (Habakkuk 2:4b). He then grew in his relationship with God. Habakkuk prophesied to Judah during the reign of Josiah that began in 2 Kings 22. **Note:** We should be as bold as Habakkuk. When we have a problem or a question, we should take it to God and wait for Him to answer.

Habakkuk is known as the prophet who asked God why—and God answered.

The Prophet Habakkuk.

The book of Zephaniah begins with, "The word of the Lord which came unto Zephaniah …" More is told of the lineage of this prophet than any other. He was the descendant of good King Hezekiah. Zephaniah boldly preached of the great apostasy in the nation. He warned of the coming judgment of God (1:17) against Judah (by the Babylonian captivity). But one day God would bring healing and restoration (3:19–21). While Zephaniah preached during the reign of King Josiah (a godly king), great reforms (destroying of idols and cleansing of the temple to restore true worship) took place. Zephaniah prophesied to Judah during the reign of Josiah that began in 2 Kings 22.

Notice the kind of influence the preaching of Zephaniah had upon King Josiah. "1. Josiah was eight years old when he began to reign, and he reigned in Jerusalem one and thirty years. 2. And he did that which was right in the sight of the LORD, and walked in the ways of David his father, and declined neither to the right hand, nor to the left" (2 Chronicles 34:1–2). We can have a great influence on others.

Zephaniah wrote of God's judgment and mercy.

2. Prophets to Israel

The book of Hosea begins with, "The word of the Lord that came unto Hosea …" God told Hosea to take a wife of the land. The wife he took and the relationship (and family) that ensued was a perfect picture of the relationship that Israel had become to God. When Hosea understood, he cried for the people to return to the Lord. "Come, and let us return unto the LORD: for he hath torn, and he will heal us; he hath smitten, and he will bind us up" (Hosea 6:1). Hosea prophesied to Israel during the reign of Uzziah (Azariah) that began in 2 Kings 15. Hosea had a life experience as a prophecy to the people.

Hosea revealed the love of God, in spite of spiritual adultery.

Amos was called to be a prophet, specifically, in Amos 7:14–15. He was only a herdsman, yet when God called him, he obeyed God. He told of the impending judgment on the surrounding nations, ending with the judgment that would fall on Israel for their sins against God (Amos 2:6–16). He asked a pertinent question. "Can two walk together, except they be agreed?" (Amos 3:3). He encouraged the people to seek the Lord. He spoke of the righteousness of God. Amos prophesied to Israel during the reign of Jeroboam II that began in 2 Kings 14:16.

NOTE

We should consider Amos's question ourselves. We cannot live as the world lives if it is not in agreement with how God wants His people to live.

Amos is known as a prophet from the country.

3. Prophets to Other Lands

Obadiah is the shortest book in the Old Testament. It was written to the descendants of Esau, the Edomites (Genesis 36:1). Remember that Esau was the twin brother of Jacob. You can see the hatred the Edomites had for the Israelites in Obadiah 1:10–14. It was because of their pride that God brought them down. "3. The pride of thine heart hath deceived thee ... that saith in his heart, Who shall bring me down to the ground? 4. Though thou exalt thyself as the eagle, and though thou set thy nest among the stars, thence will I bring thee down, saith the LORD" (Obadiah 1:3–4). Because they took pleasure in the troubles of Israel, God would deal with them (Obadiah 1:15). Obadiah prophesied to Edom, but no one is sure when it was written.

NOTE "Pride goeth before destruction, and an haughty spirit before a fall" (Proverbs 16:18).

Obadiah was written as a warning to those who persecute Israelites.

The book of Jonah begins with, "Now the word of the Lord came unto Jonah ..." Jonah is probably one of the most familiar minor prophets of the Old Testament. Jonah was a reluctant prophet to a Gentile nation, known as an enemy of God's people. He was a prophet who disobeyed God's command to go. Instead, he ran from God. Jesus referred to the experience of Jonah in the whale's belly as an illustration of his own death, burial, and resurrection (Matthew 12:40). Jonah prophesied to Nineveh (in Assyria) about the time of 2 Kings 14.

Jonah is a great picture of God saving us from ourselves and the consequences of sin when we refuse to obey God's call on our lives.

Jonah is known as an unwilling or reluctant prophet.

The book of Nahum takes place over one hundred years after Jonah. Nineveh was the world's greatest city at this time in history. Although the nation repented in Jonah's time, they had reverted back to their sin, falling even deeper. "The LORD is slow to anger, and great in power, and will not at all acquit the wicked: ..." (Nahum 1:3a). Nineveh, a greatly fortified city, was utterly destroyed. Nahum prophesied of Assyria about the time of 2 Kings 21.

Nahum is known as one who prophesied the destruction of Nineveh.

In Conclusion:

Respond when God calls. It may be a minor thing in your eyes that God asks of you but very important to the kingdom of God. The prophets came from all walks of life. God used them where they were or sent them where He needed them. Each of these prophets recognized the sovereignty of God in all areas of life.

NOTE

Amos, a herdsman (Amos 7:14), was not educated in the school of prophets.

Micah, a rustic from an obscure town twenty-five miles southwest of Jerusalem, preached to the poor and oppressed.

Zephaniah was a descendant of King Hezekiah.

BIBLE ORDER	POSSIBLE HISTORICAL ORDER
Hosea	Joel
Joel	Jonah
Amos	Amos
Obadiah	Hosea
Jonah	Micah
Micah	Nahum
Nahum	Zephaniah
Habakkuk	Habakkuk
Zephaniah	Obadiah

Reinforcement:

Remember what happened to Jonah when he tried to run away from what God asked him to do? Jonah is a great picture of God saving us from ourselves and the consequences of sin when we refuse to obey God's call on our lives. We should learn to obey our authorities that we can hear with our ears. In doing that, we will be more able to hear from God that we cannot hear with our ears, only our hearts. If we don't learn to obey those in authority over us that we can see and hear, chances are we will never "hear" God, much less obey Him, in our spiritual lives.

Closing:

It would be good to close with a short prayer reinforcing today's lesson. Always include any prayer requests you may have. Today, pray, asking God to help us learn to always obey His voice.

LESSON 10

Nine Pre–Exile Minor Prophets:
Hosea to Zephaniah

Match the scripture verse on the left with the phrase you think it means, listed on the right. **Learn to obey God's words!**

1. Philippians 2:14

a. Think on things that are true, honest, just, and pure.

2. Ephesians 6:1–3

b. Do your job without arguing or complaining.

3. Exodus 20:17

c. Love the Lord God and your neighbor as yourself.

4. Philippians 4:8

d. Don't be foolish; be wise.

5. Ephesians 4:25

e. Tell the truth; don't lie.

6. James 4:17

f. Children do what your parents tell you to do.

7. Ephesians 5:15

g. Don't want things that belong to others.

8. Luke 10:27

h. Choose not to sin; do what is right.

Remember: the prophets were just ordinary men who obeyed God's Word.

Answers: 1. b; 2. f; 3. g; 4. a; 5. e; 6. h; 7. d; 8. c

THREE POST-EXILE MINOR PROPHETS: HAGGAI TO MALACHI

Key Verse

Therefore say thou unto them, Thus saith the LORD of hosts; Turn ye unto me, saith the LORD of hosts, and I will turn unto you, saith the LORD of hosts.

— ZECHARIAH 1:3

Key Verse Thought: Review the key verse. We must choose whether or not we will obey what God's Word teaches. Think for a minute. "What happens when you make a wrong turn in traffic? Can you get lost if you are traveling a new road and take a wrong turn?" In life, we can't always see what is ahead. If we make a wrong turn, we need to immediately correct our course. Today, we see words of warning and encouragement from the prophets. (Refer to key verse.) They echo a call from God for the people to return to Him, and He will turn to them.

Emphasis: We must choose to turn to God and not the things of the world.

Lesson Summary: Today we look at the last three books of prophecy (Haggai, Zechariah, and Malachi), which are post-exile—after the people were carried away captive and had returned to their homeland. These books take place in history during the time of Ezra, Nehemiah, and Esther. Once they returned, they had an important task ahead of them, but they quickly became tired. God sent prophets to tell the people that God should be first and foremost in their lives. These prophets also, once again, reminded the people of the importance of fearing God and obeying His commands. They are reminded of the promise that the Messiah is coming and that God isn't finished with His people yet. The Old Testament ends with a warning of a curse for those who do not remember the words of the Law and the prophets.

Suggested Bible Reading to Prepare for This Lesson

- ⊘ Monday: **Haggai 1; 2**
- ⊘ Tuesday: **Zachariah 1–4**
- ⊘ Wednesday: **Zechariah 5; 6**
- ⊘ Thursday: **Zechariah 8–10**
- ⊘ Friday: **Zechariah 12–14**
- ⊘ Saturday: **Malachi 4**

Three Post-Exile Minor Prophets:
Haggai to Malachi

1 ## Haggai

- A prophet who reminded the people that God comes first
- Prophesied to the returning remnant during the leadership of Zerubbabel

2 ## Zechariah

- Also a priest; prophesied to the returning remnant during the leadership of Zerubbabel
- Encouraged the people to finish; God's not finished with them yet
- Saw many visions of prophecy

3 ## Malachi

- Known as the last call to return to God before a four-hundred-year silence
- A last prophetic call, ending the Old Testament with a curse (about a century after the return)

MAIESTAS DOMINI
INGRESSA EST
TEMPLVM

1. Haggai

Haggai prophesied to the remnant that had returned after the Babylonian captivity. The people had left a life of luxury in Babylon for a land that had lain nearly desolate for seventy years. The people began rebuilding the temple but quit. They built their own homes and failed to complete God's temple. Haggai had a message for the people. "Go up to the mountain, and bring wood, and build the house; and I will take pleasure in it, and I will be glorified, saith the LORD" (Haggai 1:8). Within three weeks of Haggai's first message, Zerubbabel, Joshua (the son of the high priest), and the people were "stirred" to begin the completion of the temple (Haggai 1:14).

Haggai, Zerubbabel, and Joshua

Haggai is known as a prophet who reminded the people that God comes first.

2. Zechariah

Zechariah was a priest and prophet. He prophesied at the same time as Haggai and kind of supplemented what Haggai was saying to the people. He especially had words of encouragement for Zerubbabel (one who helped lead the people to finish rebuilding the temple). "6. Then he answered and spake unto me, saying, This is the word of the LORD unto Zerubbabel, saying, Not by might, nor by power, but by my spirit, saith the LORD of hosts. ... 9. The hands of Zerubbabel have laid the foundation of this house; his hands shall also finish it; and thou shalt know that the LORD of hosts hath sent me unto you" (Zechariah 4:6, 9).

When God asks His people to do something, He gives them the strength and encouragement to complete it.

Zechariah had a message of encouragement to the people as well. He wanted to let the people know that God was not finished with His people yet. He had many mighty plans in store.

Zechariah saw many visions. Among the most familiar were a man with a measuring line, Joshua with the filthy garments, and the flying scroll. Isaiah was the Major Prophet with the most prophecies about Christ, and Zechariah was the Minor Prophet with the most prophecies about Christ.

Zechariah encouraged the people to finish; God wasn't finished with them yet.

3. Malachi

Malachi prophesied about one hundred years after Haggai and Zechariah, just before the four hundred years of silence. The people had once again turned from God, falling deeply into sin. They no longer obeyed God's commands. God had a poignant question for them. "A son honoureth his father, and a servant his master: if then I be a father, where is mine honour? and if I be a master, where is my fear? saith the LORD of hosts unto you, O priests, that despise my name. And ye say, Wherein have we despised thy name?" (Malachi 1:6). The people needed the prophets to tell them how far they had fallen from God's Word.

Once again, God let them know that "...the Lord, whom they seek, shall suddenly come to his temple..." (Malachi 3:1), a reminder that the Messiah (Jesus) was coming soon. Malachi was a last prophetic call, ending the Old Testament with a promise of a curse for those who reject God's Word.

Malachi was known as the last call to return to God before a four-hundred-year silence.

A Deeper Path:

Understand the importance of a right relationship with others. It is a picture of our relationship with God. God compares His relationship with Christians to a parent/child relationship throughout the Bible. He wants to be our loving Father, if only we will obey Him.

Reinforcement:

When the people went back to their homeland, they still failed to always do what God asked them to do. They needed reminding, just as we do. When we disobey God's commands, we need to immediately tell God we are sorry and not do it again (repent). It is a daily task to commit to live a life pleasing to God.

Think about how faithful they were in their walk with God. Do you have Jesus in your heart? (If you are teaching a group, be ready, as a teacher, to briefly share the plan of salvation. To remember, see lesson 8 for the Roman's Road verses.) If you are a Christian, do you read your Bible? Do you obey what it says in God's Word? Do you realize when you are doing wrong? How is your relationship with your family? Answering some of these questions helps you take a look at your own heart and life. God does—daily (remember Job 7:17–18).

Closing:

It would be good to close with a short prayer reinforcing today's lesson. Always include any prayer requests you may have. *Today, pray for God to help us know where we have failed His Word. Ask God for help to correct our courses, so we do not make wrong turns or wrong choices.*

LESSON 11

Three Post-Exile Minor Prophets:
Haggai to Malachi

Directions: Match the book with the scripture. If you can't remember, look in your Bible.

1. Haggai 1:8

a. "A son honoureth his father, and a servant his master: if then I be a father, where is mine honour? and if I be a master, where is my fear? saith the LORD of hosts unto you, …"

2. Zechariah 4:6

b. "Go up to the mountain, and bring wood, and build the house; and I will take pleasure in it, and I will be glorified, saith the LORD."

3. Malachi 1:6

c. "Then he answered and spake unto me, saying, This is the word of the LORD unto Zerubbabel, saying, Not by might, nor by power, but by my spirit, saith the LORD of hosts."

Answers: 1. c; 2. b; 3. a

REVIEW OLD TESTAMENT DIVISIONS

Key Verse

For Ezra had prepared his heart to seek the law of the LORD, and to do it, and to teach in Israel statutes and judgments.

— EZRA 7:10

Key Verse Thought: Before beginning today's lesson, consider today's key verse. If you are teaching these lessons to a group, as a teacher, you should adhere to this verse. We must prepare our hearts to seek the law of the Lord. We must live it out in our lives and then proceed to tell others. Emphasize to students that each person who has Jesus in his or her heart must do the same as the above. We need to prepare our hearts to seek and know God's Word. We must obey it. Then we will be able to teach others—first by the way we live our lives and then by being a verbal witness to others. It must happen in this order, just as we see it in Ezra 7:10. It is important to know God's Word. That is why we are studying it in detail.

Emphasis: We need to prepare our hearts to seek and know God's Word.

Lesson Summary: As this is a review, encourage your students (if you are teaching a group) to do most of the "telling" this week. Encourage them to unload all the knowledge they have of the Old Testament on you. This will also help you, as the teacher, to know where your class's deficiencies are in Old Testament knowledge. Then you can focus more on your class's needs.

If you are teaching a group, first have your students (or do so yourself if you're not in a group setting) find Esther 10 in their Bibles and hold Genesis through Esther 10 in their left hands. Next, have them hold the rest of the Old Testament (Job to Malachi) in their right hands. Emphasize that everything in their right hands takes place within the time frame that their left hands are holding.

Suggested Bible Reading to Prepare for This Lesson

- ⊘ Monday: **Colossians 1**
- ⊘ Tuesday: **Genesis 6–9**
- ⊘ Wednesday: **1 Samuel 8**
- ⊘ Thursday: **2 Kings 21**
- ⊘ Friday: **2 Samuel 7**
- ⊘ Saturday: **Revelation 1**

Review and be prepared to share about the following, looking back to lesson 4 for additional information.

Review Old Testament Divisions

1 **Law (Pentateuch)—Five**
- Genesis to Deuteronomy
- All historical books
- Five pre-Canaan history books

2 **Historical Books—Twelve**
- Joshua to Esther
- Joshua to 2 Chronicles; reveals history while Canaan is occupied—nine occupied
- Ezra to Esther; reveals history after expulsion from Canaan — three post-exile

3 **Personal Books—Five**
- Job to Song of Solomon
- Individual and experiential books
- Deal with problems of the individual heart and written as poems

4 **Major Prophets—Five**
- Isaiah to Daniel—prophetic
- Isaiah and Jeremiah—pre-exile
- Lamentations and Ezekiel—intermediate; begin in homeland and are carried captive
- Daniel—exile

⑤ Minor Prophets—Twelve

- Hosea to Malachi—prophetic
- Hosea to Zephaniah—nine pre-exile
- Haggai to Malachi—three post-exile

Ideas for Review for a Class Setting

- Call out an Old Testament book and have students tell you in which division it is found.
- Have them tell you what each book is about.
- Let them tell you a story, event, or person from each book. (Be prepared to tell one if no one has one.)
- Have Old Testament Bible drills (race to see who can find a particular book first).
- Use any (or all) of the resource reviews you have made.

Above all, encourage students to want to know the Bible!

Closing:

It would be good to close with a short prayer reinforcing today's lesson. Always include any prayer requests you may have. *Today, pray for God to help us want to know God's Word so we can be a living and a verbal witness for Him.*

LESSON 12

Review Old Testament Divisions

1. What is the first division? _____

Write the names of the five books. _____

_____

_____

What were these books about? _____

2. What is the second division? _____

Write the names of the twelve books. _____

_____

_____

3. What is the third division? _____

_____ Write the names of the five books.

_____

What were these books about? _____

_____

4. What is the fourth division? _____

_____ Write the names of the five books.

_____

_____

5. What is the fifth division? _____

Write the names of the twelve books. _____

_____

_____

_____

_____

Answers:

1. Law (Pentateuch); Genesis, Exodus, Leviticus, Numbers, Deuteronomy; Moses recorded these books, recording of the first 2500 years of history, sin enter into the world, causing separation from God, yet God actively involved in men's lives.

2. Historical Books; Joshua, Judges, Ruth, 1 Samuel, 2 Samuel, 1 Kings, 2 Kings, 1 Chronicles, 2 Chronicles, Ezra, Nehemiah, Esther; the conquering of the Promised Land, the time of judges, the people desiring an earthly king , the kingdom divided, carried captive to other lands, the people return to Israel;

3. Personal Books; Job, Psalms, Proverbs, Ecclesiastes, Song of Solomon; written as poems, deal with individuals' very personal experiences with God, and individual's heart issues as they seek to know and understand God better;

4. Major Prophets; Isaiah, Jeremiah, Lamentations, Ezekiel, Daniel;

5. Minor Prophets; Hosea, Joel, Amos, Obadiah, Jonah, Micah, Nahum, Habakkuk, Zephaniah, Haggai, Zechariah, Malachi

JESUS IN THE OLD TESTAMENT

How Jesus Relates to the Old Testament

LESSON 13

Key Verse

Think not that I am come to destroy the law, or the prophets: I am not come to destroy, but to fulfill.

— MATTHEW 5:17

Key Verse Thought: Read today's key verse. You may understand it better with the following: Fulfilled means "to fill out; complete or made them perfect; to accomplish an end." Jesus came to complete the promise God made to Adam and Eve (and all of mankind) in the garden after they sinned. When Jesus came, He did not take away the importance of the Old Testament law and prophets, for He accomplished what God required of Him. So when Jesus came, He did not take away the importance of the Old Testament Law and Prophets; instead He fulfilled the words spoken and preached, which allowed Him to be the perfect sacrifice to appease the wrath of a just and righteous God.

Emphasis: When Jesus came, He did not take away the importance of the Old Testament Law Prophets; instead, He fulfilled them. This means He completed them, or made them completely perfect.

Lesson Summary: Jesus came to fulfill the Law and the words of the prophets. He did just that. You will find a page in your book at the end of this lesson, listing at least one verse from each of the Old Testament books that was a prophecy of Jesus that He fulfilled. We will go over only one verse for each of the five divisions we have studied in the last few lessons. (We will eventually cover the rest of them.) It would be good to keep that page handy for future reference.

Suggested Bible Reading to Prepare for This Lesson

- Monday: **Deuteronomy 18**
- Tuesday: **John 5**
- Wednesday: **John 10**
- Thursday: **John 6**
- Friday: **Zechariah 12–14**
- Saturday: **John 21**

Jesus in the Old Testament
How Jesus Relates to the Old Testament

1 **The Law**

- The Law and the Prophet — Deuteronomy 18:15
- John 5:46

2 **History**

- The King, Son of David — 2 Samuel 7:12–14a
- Romans 1:3 – 4

3 **Personal**

- Our Great Shepherd — Psalm 23
- John 10:14–15

4 **Major Prophets**

- Son of God Who Would Come — Daniel 3:25; 9:25
- John 6:35–40, 45

5   **Minor Prophets**

- He Whom They Pierced — Zechariah 12:10
- Luke 24:25–27; John 19:34

To help understand the importance of this lesson, read the following scriptures:

44. And he said unto them, These are the words which I spake unto you, while I was yet with you, that all things must be fulfilled, which were written in the law of Moses, and in the prophets, and in the psalms, concerning me. 45. Then opened he their understanding, that they might understand the scriptures, 46. And said unto them, Thus it is written, and thus it behoved Christ to suffer, and to rise from the dead the third day: 47. And that repentance and remission of sins should be preached in his name among all nations, beginning at Jerusalem. 48. And ye are witnesses of these things. (Luke 24:44–48)

1. The Law and the Prophet

Moses Breaks the Tables of the Law.

- "The LORD thy God will raise up unto thee a Prophet from the midst of thee, of thy brethren, like unto me; unto him ye shall hearken" (Deuteronomy 18:15).

- "For had ye believed Moses, ye would have believed me: for he wrote of me (Jesus)" (John 5:46).

2. The King, Son of David

- "12. And when thy days be fulfilled, and thou shalt sleep with thy fathers, I will set up thy seed after thee, which shall proceed out of thy bowels, and I will establish his kingdom. 13. He shall build an house for my name, and I will stablish the throne of his kingdom for ever. 14. I will be his father, and he shall be my son…" (2 Samuel 7:12–14a).

- "3. Concerning his Son Jesus Christ our Lord, which was made of the seed of David according to the flesh; 4. And declared to be the Son of God with power, according to the spirit of holiness, by the resurrection from the dead" (Romans 1:3–4).

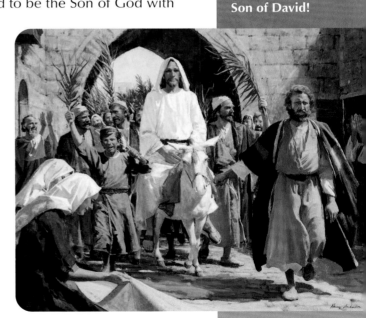

Hosanna to the Son of David!

3. Our Great Shepherd

The Lord is my Good Shepherd.

- "1. The LORD is my shepherd; I shall not want. 2. He maketh me to lie down in green pastures: he leadeth me beside the still waters. 3. He restoreth my soul: he leadeth me in the paths of righteousness for his name's sake. 4. Yea, though I walk through the valley of the shadow of death, I will fear no evil: for thou art with me; thy rod and thy staff they comfort me. 5. Thou preparest a table before me in the presence of mine enemies: thou anointest my head with oil; my cup runneth over. 6. Surely goodness and mercy shall follow me all the days of my life: and I will dwell in the house of the LORD for ever" (Psalm 23:1-6).

- "14. I am the good shepherd, and know my sheep, and am known of mine. 15. As the Father knoweth me, even so know I the Father: and I lay down my life for the sheep" (John 10:14–15).

4. Son of God Who Would Come

- "He answered and said, Lo, I see four men loose, walking in the midst of the fire, and they have no hurt; and the form of the fourth is like the Son of God" (Daniel 3:25).

- "Know therefore and understand, that from the going forth of the commandment to restore and to build Jerusalem unto the Messiah the Prince shall be seven weeks, and threescore and two weeks: the street shall be built again, and the wall, even in troublous times" (Daniel 9:25).

- "35. And Jesus said unto them, I am the bread of life: he that cometh to me shall never hunger; and he that believeth on me shall never thirst. 36. But I said unto you, That ye also have seen me, and believe not. 37. All that the Father giveth me shall come to me; and him that cometh to me I will in no wise cast out. 38. For I came down from heaven, not to do mine own will, but the will of him that sent me. 39. And this is the Father's will which hath sent me, that of all which he hath given me I should lose nothing, but should raise it up again at the last day. 40. And this is the will of him that sent me, that every one which seeth the Son, and believeth on him, may have everlasting life: and I will raise him up at the last day" (John 6:35–40).

- "It is written in the prophets, And they shall be all taught of God. Every man therefore that hath heard, and hath learned of the Father, cometh unto me" (John 6:45).

5. He Whom They Pierced

- "And I will pour upon the house of David, and upon the inhabitants of Jerusalem, the spirit of grace and of supplications: and they shall look upon me whom they have pierced, and they shall mourn for him, as one mourneth for his only son, and shall be in bitterness for him, as one that is in bitterness for his firstborn" (Zechariah 12:10).

- "25. Then he said unto them, O fools, and slow of heart to believe all that the prophets have spoken: 26. Ought not Christ to have suffered these things, and to enter into his glory? 27. And beginning at Moses and all the prophets, he expounded unto them in all the scriptures the things concerning himself" (Luke 24:25–27).

- "But one of the soldiers with a spear pierced his side, and forth with came there out blood and water" (John 19:34).

In Conclusion

There was a great plot to kill Paul because he lived as a Christian, preaching Jesus to the lost. Paul, the apostle, used this in his defense before Festus. "But this I confess unto thee, that after the way which they call heresy, so worship I the God of my fathers, believing all things which are written in the law and in the prophets" (Acts 24:14).

He believed all things that are written in the Law and the Prophets. Do you?

Reinforcement:

Remember the importance of being in a Bible study and reading God's Word, so you can learn about Jesus. Make it your goal to let the Old Testament become much more to you than a collection of stories about people who lived long ago. In this study, you will search and find out why these people wanted to obey God and how they knew He would one day send Jesus. These events will be an encouragement to you that God is with you and takes care of His people.

Closing:

It would be good to close with a short prayer reinforcing today's lesson. Always include any prayer requests you may have. Today, be encouraged to pray for God to help us believe every word recorded in the Law and Prophets and to want to trust in Jesus.

Jesus in the Old Testament

Genesis	-The Promised Seed – Genesis 3:15	
Exodus	-The Passover Lamb – Exodus 12:3, 12, 13	The Pentateuch
Leviticus	-The Scapegoat – Leviticus 16:20	The Law and The Prophet
Numbers	-The Brazen Serpent – Numbers 21:8	Deuteronomy 18:15
Deuteronomy	-The Prophet – Deuteronomy 18:15	

Joshua	-The Captain of Our Salvation – Joshua 5:13-15	
Judges	-Our Deliverer – Judges 2:18	
Ruth	-Our Near Kinsman – Ruth 3:11-13	
1 Samuel	-Our Stone of Help – 1 Samuel 7:12	Pre-Captive History
2 Samuel	-Our King, the Son of David – 2 Samuel 7:12-14a	The King – Son of David
1 Kings	-The Fulfillment of our Hearts' Desire – 1 Kings 10:7-8	2 Samuel 7:12-14a
2 Kings	-The Hidden Treasure – 2 Kings 22:8	
1 Chronicles	-The Lion of the Tribe of Judah – 1 Chronicles 4	
2 Chronicles	-Our Hope of Returning – 2 Chronicles 30:6, 15-20	

Ezra	-The Center of Our Life: The Temple – Ezra 2:10; 6:15	Post-Captive History
Nehemiah	-Our Defense (the Walls) – Nehemiah 1:3; 6:15-16	Our Life – Ezra 1:2-3
Esther	-Our Unseen Protector – Esther 6:1-11	Jerusalem / Temple and Walls

Job	-Our Daysman – Job 9:33	
Psalms	-Our Great Shepherd of the Sheep – Psalm 23:1	Personal Books
Proverbs	-Our Wisdom – Proverbs 8:12, 34-35	Our Great Shepherd
Ecclesiastes	-Our Preacher – Ecclesiastes 12:11-12	Psalm 23
Song of Solomon	–Our Beloved – Song of Solomon 6:3	

Isaiah	-The Suffering Servant – Isaiah 53	
Jeremiah	-Our Potter – Jeremiah 18:1-6	Major Prophets
Lamentations	-Our Hope of Salvation – Lamentations 3:22-26	Son of God Who Would Come
Ezekiel	-The Son of Man – Ezekiel 12:2	Daniel 9:25
Daniel	-The Son of God – Daniel 3:25	

Hosea	-Our Hope of Resurrection – Hosea 6:2	
Joel	-Our Hope of Restoration – Joel 2:25, 32	
Amos	-The Lord of Judgment – Amos 9:1-4	
Obadiah	-Our Deliver – Obadiah 1:17	
Jonah	-Our Intercessor – Jonah 2:2	
Micah	-The Ruler from Old – Micah 5:2	
Nahum	-Our Stronghold in the Day of Trouble – Nahum 1:17	Minor Prophets
Habakkuk	-The God of our Salvation – Habakkuk 3:18	He Whom They Pierced
Zephaniah	-The Hope of the Gentiles – Zephaniah 2:1-3	Zechariah 12:10
Haggai	-The God Who is with Us – Haggai 1:13	
Zechariah	-The Branch – Zechariah 6:12	
Malachi	-The Lord Whom We Seek – Malachi 3:1	

LESSON 13

Jesus in the Old Testament
How Jesus Relates
to the Old Testament

Complete the following.

1. Who would come? (Deuteronomy 18:15) _____

_____

Who came? (John 5:46) _____

_____

2. What did God promise David? (2 Samuel 7:12–14a) _____

_____

Who came? (Romans 1:3–4) _____

_____

3. Who is Psalm 23 talking about? _____

_____

Who came? (John 10:14–15) _____

_____

4. Who was with the men in the fire? (Daniel 3:25) _____

_____

Who was promised? (Daniel 9:25) _____

_____

Who did Jesus say He was? (John 6:39–40) _____

_____

What will Jesus do for all who believe in Him? (John 6:40) _____

_____

_____

5. Who does Zechariah say would be mourned? (Zechariah 12:10)

_____

Who was the one who would suffer and be pierced? (Luke 24:25–
26 and John 19:34) _____

_____

6. Write today's key verse — Matthew 5:17. _____

_____

_____

_____ Did Jesus do what He came to do?_____

www.lighthouse.pub

Visit our website
to purchase books and preview
upcoming titles.

Contact us at:
feedback@lighthouse.pub